THE BOOK OF THE TWELVE PROPHETS

THE BOOK OF THE
TWELVE PROPHETS

Translated by

David R. Slavitt

New York   Oxford

Oxford University Press

2000

Oxford University Press

Oxford   New York
Athens   Auckland   Bangkok   Bogotá   Buenos Aires   Calcutta
Cape Town   Chennai   Dar es Salaam   Delhi   Florence   Hong Kong   Istanbul
Karachi   Kuala Lumpur   Madrid   Melbourne   Mexico City   Mumbai
Nairobi   Paris   São Paulo   Singapore   Taipei   Tokyo   Toronto   Warsaw

and associated companies in
Berlin   Ibadan

Published by Oxford University Press, Inc.
198 Madison Avenue, New York, New York 10016

Oxford is a registered trademark of Oxford University Press

Library of Congress Cataloging-in-Publicationi Data
Bible. O.T. Minor Prophets. English. Slavitt. 2000.
The book of the Twelve Prophets / translated by David R. Slavitt.
        p.   cm.
ISBN 0-19-513214-9
I. Title.
BS1560.A3S53   2000
224'.9'05209—dc21   99-28031

1   3   5   7   9   8   6   4   2

Printed in the United States of America
on acid-free paper

For Sonja and William Jay Smith

CONTENTS

INTRODUCTION

The prophets—the *nevim*—make us uncomfortable, which is part of their job. They come, or so they claim, from God with messages, often unpleasant, that they deliver to the people or, sometimes, to the king. In ancient Israel, they were on occasion consulted by individuals who simply wanted help in finding things they had lost. Prophets could be leaders of local cults or they would work solo; they behaved at times in ways that were bizarre enough so that they could be dismissed as "mad" (1 Kings 9.11). They could also serve as military advisors to the throne or they could be miracle workers, making axe heads float or calling down fire from heaven.

To make matters worse, their messages are often murky. The texts of their writings are not reliable, and there are passages from which any clear sense is difficult to extract. And the prophets, themselves, seem to have had an uneasy time with one another, and their analyses and prognostications could be inconsistent or even diametrically opposite, each of them claiming to speak the truth and accusing others of false prophecy.

To complicate matters further, the writings of the prophets are part of the Bible—a book we hold in such high esteem that we have practically forbidden its use in public education, even in the guise of "literature." To talk about holy scripture in that way would be, some people believe, disrespectful to the revealed word of God. Others, meanwhile, worry that teachers may not limit themselves to literary discussion but may advert somehow to the "meaning" or even the "truth" of the words, which would constitute a violation of the constitutionally required separation of church and state.

This book, however, is merely literary. What I have tried to do is to translate the "poetry" of the twelve "minor" prophets, and I make no claim to a secure understanding of these writings. There are passages here that I find quite mysterious. But poetry does not need to be explicated—or even capable of explication—to be effective. We can be moved by passages or even by entire poems in which our rational understanding is approximate at best. I come at these texts not as a scholar but as a poet and rhetorician, and my impudent claim is that the scholars' struggle with the meaning of these writings may be every bit as risky as my much more free-wheeling approach. The "truth" of poetry is primarily an aesthetic and emotional one, and explication often ignores and almost always betrays these vital aspects of its praxis. The writing of a poem is an act of discovery which may be incomplete but still valuable. (In fact, it can be all the more valuable for its incompleteness.)

Poets do not always understand their own poems; the reader can often be moved and delighted by poetry he or she finds "difficult," ambiguous, or even opaque.

From the time we were very young we heard and learned to love nursery rhymes, the meaning of which was impossibly remote. The connection of "Ring around the Rosie" (or "Ring-a-ring o' Roses") with the plague? That could come later, or never, but the rhyme's odd combination of cheeriness with its funereal rhythm spoke to us and still stays with us.

Auden's test for poetry was physical, even physiological. He would copy out a passage in long hand and, where his fingers hesitated, look hard at the word and the phrase to try to find out what was wrong. In other words, he trusted his nervous system to tell him what his intellect alone might not have been able to detect.

My way of working with the writings of these twelve prophets was to roll them in my mouth to discover their texture and taste, to let them resonate in my sinuses, and to see what they did to my muscles and nerves as I transcribed these stern and splendid verses into an English that was comfortable but not too comfortable—to see how they would come out.

THE PROPHETIC BOOKS OF THE Bible are divided by tradition into the "Former Prophets"—*Joshua, Judges, Samuel,* and *Kings*—which are historical books but assigned to the prophetic part of scripture in order to keep the Pentateuch in its own separate category; and the four books of the "Latter Prophets"—*Isaiah, Jeremiah, Ezekiel,* and "The Twelve," or, in Aramaic, the "Terei 'Asar." These "twelve" are sometimes distinguished as "minor" but only in the sense that their books are shorter. They were grouped together as a distinct book and were written out on a single scroll as early as the second century B.C. They include:

Hosea (eighth century B.C., during the reigns of Uzziah, Jotham, Ahaz, and Hezekiah, kings of Judah, and Jeroboam II, king of Israel). Hosea is a generation later than Amos, but his book is conventionally placed first. It is a complicated combination of the personal and the national, for God's instruction to the prophet that he should marry a prostitute provides the basis of an allegory about God's mixed feelings of love and disgust for Israel in its state of sin. The predicament of the individual becomes a figure for that of the nation, and the tensions between estrange-ment and reconciliation and between sickness and recovery (or even death and resurrection) operate on many levels.

Joel (late sixth and fifth centuries B.C.). Nothing is known about this prophet except that his name means "Yahweh is God" and that he is the son of someone named Pethuel. He is much concerned with the correctness of the obser-vances of Temple worship, which implies that there was a Temple—presumably the Second Temple of Zerubbabel. The book is divided into two parts, the first being a great description of a plague of locusts and the second being an apocalyptic vision of the Day of the Lord and a series of prophecies of salvation in which Jerusalem will be restored and the gentiles will be punished for their misdeeds.

Amos (eighth century B.C., during the reigns of Uzziah, king of Judah, and Jeroboam II, king of Israel). Amos is the earliest of the prophets to have his own book, Samuel, Elijah, and Elisha being known from the historical books of Samuel and Kings. He is earlier than Isaiah, Jeremiah, and Ezekiel, but is included in the Twelve because his book is shorter than theirs are. The original oral messages of protest against domestic wrongs and calls for reform have been edited by a skillful hand into a coherent literary composition that gives us a rounded representation of Amos' life and work.

Obadiah (sixth century B.C.). With its twenty-one verses, this is the shortest book in the Bible. It announces the Lord's decision to destroy the Edomites because of their betrayal of Judah, predicts the Day of the Lord, and proclaims that the dispersed Israelites will return one day to live in Canaan.

Jonah (eighth century B.C.). This antihero is the best known of the Twelve and the most popular, no doubt because most of us would have the same kind of resistance to a divine call. Moses, Amos, and Jeremiah are also reluctant, but Jonah actually runs away. It not an altogether comforting book, however, for it demonstrates the shifting standards by which we are to judge the words of prophets—predictions of the destruction of nations may be accurate, but the situation may change as the Lord's mind is swayed by his pity and compassion.

Micah (eighth century B.C., during the reigns of Kings Jotham, Ahaz, and Hezekiah of Judah). This name is a shortened form of Micaiah, which means "Who is like Yahweh?" He seems to have been a contemporary of Isaiah, but was a man of the country—a tiny village in the Judean foothills—rather than an aristocratic city dweller. He speaks out against social injustice and his words seem to have been changed and adapted to fit later conditions. I have confined myself to what is presumably from the prophet himself and have omitted the later interpolations.

Nahum (seventh century B.C.). His name means "comfort" although his book is a violent description of vengeance and a portrayal of the last days of Assyria's capital, Nineveh, which was destroyed in 612 B.C. by the Babylonians. The good news of Nineveh's fall turned out to be a disappointment when the Egyptians and the Babylonians took over as masters of the region and were even worse than the Assyrians. (Nahum 1.2–8 is an incomplete acrostic, which I have tried to render in English.)

Habakkuk (seventh century B.C.) is a prophet in whom there is a struggle between despair and hope, and hope wins in a splendid declaration of faith with which the book concludes. The description of the appearance of the Lord is one of the high points of all Hebrew literature.

Zephaniah (seventh century B.C., in the reign of King Josiah). This prophet, whose name means "God protects," delivers a message very like that of Isaiah, speaking out against pride as treacherous and conducive to rebellion against God's authority. The book is a dramatic dialogue in seven parts between God and an interlocutor, presumably the prophet. It has been observed that this book opens the door to the messages of the following three books which have to do with the rebuilding of the temple and the fate of Israel in exile.

Haggai (520 B.C. in the reign of Darius, King of Persia). Haggai's name means that he was born on a feast day, just as Shabbetai is often used as the name for one who has been born on a Sabbath. Haggai has been compared to Moses in that he oversaw the return from an exile. His prophecy is about the necessity for Zerubbabel, the governor, and Joshua, the high priest to begin work on the rebuilding of the temple. To the objection that the people are too poor for such an undertaking, Haggai's reply is that the reason they are poor is that they have not rebuilt the temple.

Zechariah (520–518 B.C. in the reign of Darius, King of Persia). This is a series of visions and oracles that demonstrates how what is happening on earth is a reflection or projection of what is taking place in heaven. There are warnings against the sins of pre-exilic times and a prediction (which, alas, turns out not to have been correct) that the fasts for the fall of Jerusalem (Tish'a b'Av and the Fast of Gedaliah) will now be replaced by joyful festivals of celebration. Chapters nine through fourteen make no reference to the rebuilding of the Temple or the time of Darius I, and seem clearly to have been added at another time and by another hand, and I have omitted them.)

Malachi (mid fifth century B.C.). His name means "my messenger" and it is not clear whether this is the person or the office. The book is concerned with the forms of Temple worship and obedience to the word of God. It predicts the coming of a day of judgment and ends with a vision of the return of Elijah to announce its arrival.

THE BOOK OF THE TWELVE PROPHETS

HOSEA

The word of the Lord that came to Hosea, the son of Beeri,
in the days of Uzziah, Jotham, Ahaz, and Hezekiah,
kings of Judah, and in the days of Jeroboam, the son of
Joash, king of Israel:

When the Lord first spoke through Hosea, the Lord said to
him, Go marry a whore and have children of harlotry,
for the land commits great foulness in forsaking the
Lord. So he went and took Gomer, who belonged to
Diblaim, and she conceived and bore him a son.

And the Lord told him, Call him Jezreel, which means God
sows, for soon I will punish the house of Jehu for its
bloodshed at the valley of Jezreel, and I will destroy
the kingdom of the house of Israel and break its
strength in Jezreel.

She conceived again and bore a daughter, and God said to
    him, Call her Lo-ruhamah, which means Not pitied,
    for I will have no more pity on the house of Israel but
    I will destroy them utterly. But I will have mercy on
    the house of Judah and will save them, not by bow nor
    by sword nor by horses and horsemen, and not by
    war, but by the Lord their God.

When she had weaned Lo-ruhamah, she conceived and
    bore a son, and God said, Call him Lo-ammi, which
    means Not my people, for you are not my people and
    I am not your God.

Yet shall the number of the children of Israel be as the sand
    of the sea which cannot be measured or numbered,
    and it shall come to pass that in the place where it was
    said to them, You are not my people, it shall be said to
    them, You are the sons of the living God.

Then shall the children of Judah and the children of Israel
    be gathered together and they shall appoint for
    themselves one head, and they shall come up from the
    lands, for great shall be the day of Jezreel.

2

Jezreel then shall call his brother, Ammi, My people, and
    he shall call his sister, Ruhama, She who has been
    pitied.

Plead with your mother, plead—for she is not my wife and
I am not her husband—that she stop painting her face
for whoring and perfuming her breasts for adultery,
lest I strip her naked as the day she was born and make
her like a desert, like a parched land, and kill her with
thirst.

I will not have mercy on her children for they are the
children of whoring. Their mother has worked the
streets. She who conceived them has behaved
shamefully, saying I will go and pick up men who give
me my bread and water, my wool and flax, my oil and
wine.

Therefore, watch as I block her way with thorns and make
a hedge through which she cannot find any path. She
shall run after her lovers but not overtake them. She
shall seek her Johns but not find them. And then she
shall say, "I will go back to my first husband for it was
better with me then than now."

For she had no idea that it was I who gave her the corn and
the wine and the oil, and the hoard of silver and gold
they used for the worship of Báal. And therefore I will
take back my grain in its time, and my wine in its
season, and I will take away my wool and flax that
were to cover her nakedness.

I will bare her lewdness in the sight of her lovers and no
one shall rescue her from my hand.

I will end her days of mirth, her feasts, her new moons, her
   sabbaths, and her celebrations. I will destroy her vines
   and her fig trees of which she said, "These are the loot
   my lovers have given me," and I will make them a
   jungle and the beasts of the field shall hunt in them.

I will punish her for the feast days of Báal on which she
   burned incense and decked herself out with earrings
   and jewelry and went out whoring and forgot me, says
   the Lord. You watch how I will seduce her back and
   bring her out into the wilderness and speak sweetly to
   her.

And there I will give her vineyards and make the valley of
   Achor a gate of hope, and she shall sing there as in the
   days of her youth, as she did in the day when she came
   up out of the land of Egypt.

And on that day, says the Lord, she shall call me husband
   and forget about Báal, for I will remove the names of
   Báal from her mouth and she shall speak them no
   more.

And on that day I will make a covenant with the beasts of
   the field and the birds of the heavens, and with
   crawling creatures of the ground: I will abolish the
   bow and the sword and war from the land, and I will
   make you lie down in safety, and I will betroth you to
   me forever.

I will betroth you to me in righteousness and justice and
steadfast love and mercy. I will betroth you to me in
faithfulness, and you shall know the Lord. And it shall
happen on that day, the Lord says, I will hear the
heavens and they shall hear the earth, and the earth
shall hear the corn and the wine and the oil, and they
shall hear Jezreel.

I will sow her for myself in the earth and I will have mercy
on her who has not had mercy, and I will say to Lo-
ammi, You are my people, and he shall say, You are
my God.

3

Then the Lord said to me, Go again and make love to a
woman who dotes on her pimp and is an adulteress, so
that you do what the Lord does, loving the people of
Israel even when they turn to other gods and carouse
with them and guzzle wine by the flagon.

So I found one and bought her for fifteen silver shekels and
a bushel and a peck of barley. And I told her, You
shall stay with me for many days and not be unfaithful
and not be with any other man, and I will be faithful
to you.

For the children of Israel shall have to endure many days
without a king or prince and without sacrificial altars
and without vestments and icons. And then the
children of Israel shall return and seek the Lord their
God, and David their king, and they shall hold the
Lord and his goodness in awe in the days to come.

4

Hear the word of the Lord, O people of Israel, for the Lord
has a quarrel with the inhabitants of the land because
there is no truth or mercy or knowledge of God in the
land, but instead there is false swearing and lying,
killing, theft, and adultery—violations of all law and
murder following upon murder.

Therefore the land mourns and all who dwell in it languish,
and the beasts of the field suffer and the birds of the
sky, and even the fishes of the sea shall disappear.

But let no man argue and let no one accuse another, for my
quarrel is with you, O priest. You shall stumble every
day and the prophet shall stumble every night with
you, and you shall destroy your mother, Israel.

My people are ruined for lack of knowledge because you
have rejected learning, and therefore I reject you from
being my priest. You have forgotten the law of your
God and I will therefore forget your children.

The better your lives, the more you have sinned against
    me, and therefore I will change your pride to shame.
    You batten on the sin of my people and you set their
    hearts on iniquity.

But it shall be like people, like priest: for I will punish them
    for their ways and requite them for their evil deeds.
    They shall eat and still feel hunger. They shall devote
    themselves to lust but remain childless, because they
    have forsaken the Lord and taken up harlotry.
    Whoredom and wine have driven them crazy.

My people consult wooden objects and cast sticks for their
    oracles, for a devotion to whoredom has led them
    astray. They have left their God to dally with whores.
    They sacrifice on mountain tops and make offerings in
    the hills in groves of oak and poplar and elm, because
    their shade is good.

Therefore your daughters go on the stroll and your brides
    commit adultery. I will not punish your daughters
    when they solicit like whores, nor your brides when
    they commit adultery, for there are men going with
    them, sacrificing with prostitute priestesses. And a
    deluded people shall come to ruin and play the whore.

O Israel, do not transgress and do not enter into Gilgal, or
    go up to Beth-aven, and do not swear, As the Lord
    lives.

Israel is balky as a stubborn heifer. Can the Lord feed Israel
like a docile lamb in a broad meadow?

Ephraim is committed to idolatry. Leave him with his band
of drunkards. Their wine has gone sour and they have
given themselves up to endless whoredom. Her rulers
prefer depravity to glory.

When the wind has wrapped their shame in its wings, they
shall be mortified because of their idolatry.

5

Listen, O priests, and give ear, O house of Israel. Give
heed, you in the palace, for this time judgment is on
you. You have been a snare at Mizpah, and a net
spread on Tabor, and you have dug a deep pit at
Shittim, and you have ignored my constant correction.

I know Ephraim, and Israel is not concealed from me. O
Ephraim, you have played the whore, and Israel has
become defiled.

You cannot change your behavior and return to your God,
for the spirit of whoredom is in you, and you have not
known the Lord.

The arrogance of Israel condemns itself, and therefore shall
Israel and Ephraim fall in their guilt and Judah shall
stumble with them.

With their flocks and rich herds, they shall seek the Lord,
  but they will not find him, for he has withdrawn from
  them. They have dealt falsely with the Lord, and have
  begotten alien children, and now a new moon shall
  rise to devour them with their wealth.

Blow the trumpet in Gibeah and the clarion in Ramah.
  Sound the tocsin at Beth-aven, and tremble, O
  Benjamin!

Ephraim shall be ruined in that day of judgment: among the
  tribes of Israel, I declare what shall surely come to pass.

The princes of Judah were like those who remove
  boundary lines. I will pour out my wrath on them like
  a flood.

Ephraim is oppressed and broken in judgment because he
  pursued what was worthless. I will be to Ephraim like
  pus, and I will ruin Judah's house like dry rot.

When Ephraim realised he was sick and Judah saw that he
  was covered with sores, Ephraim went to Assyria to
  their Great King, but he has no power to heal your
  wounds.

I will be to Ephraim as a lion and I will be a fierce lion cub
  to the house of Judah. I will maul and tear and carry
  off, and none shall be able to rescue him.

I will return to my place until they acknowledge their guilt
and seek my countenance, and in their distress seek
me, saying,

6

Come, let us return to the Lord, for he who has torn us will
heal us. He who has wounded us will bind up our
wounds. After two days, he will revive us, and on the
third day he will raise us up, and we shall live again in
his sight.

Then we shall know if we follow on the path to knowledge
of the Lord whose going forth is sure as dawn, and
who comes to us as showers in the spring that water
the earth.

O Ephraim, what shall I do with you? How shall I deal
with you, Judah? Your virtue is like a morning mist
and in the heat of the day it disappears.

Therefore have I excoriated you with my prophets and
lacerated you with my words. My judgment shines
forth like light. Love is what I want more than
sacrifice, and the knowledge of God more than burnt
offerings.

At Atmah, they have broken the covenant and dealt falsely
with me. Gilead is a den of wickedness, fouled by
bloodshed. As a gang of robbers waits for a victim, so
the company of priests joins together to commit
murder on the road to Shechem. Their behavior is an
outrage.

In Israel's sanctuary, I have seen horrible things. Ephraim's
harlotry is there and Israel is defiled. And for you,
Judah, there comes a harvest of reckoning . . .

7

. . . when I would have healed Israel, but then the guilt of
Ephraim is revealed and the wicked deeds of Samaria.
They have broken faith.

The thief breaks in and outside the band of robbers lays in
wait, not thinking that I know all their evil doing. But
their crimes engulf them and are staring me in the
face.

They anoint kings with their wickedness and establish
princes with their lies. They are all adulterers. They
are like an oven the baker has heated for dough he has
leavened when he no longer stirs the fire but the coals
are still hot and ready to ignite.

On the day of the king's coronation, the princes made him
sick with wine, and all those to whom he waved were
already plotting, for their hearts were like that oven
that is ready for the next day's work. The baker sleeps
but in the morning, he can fan the flames awake.

Their hearts are hot with intrigue, and all night their anger
smolders to flare up in the morning. They are all hot
as an oven and they devour their rulers. Their kings
have fallen and none of them calls upon me.

Ephraim and his foreigners are a sorry mixture. He is a half-
baked cake. Strangers sap his strength but he is
oblivious. His hair is white but he has none of the
wisdom of age.

The pride of Israel bears witness against them and they do
not return to the Lord their God or seek him for all
their trouble.

Ephraim is dumb as a chicken, stupid and without sense,
calling now on Egypt and now on Assyria for support.
Wherever they go, I will cast my net over them and
bring them down like the birds of the sky. I will
chastise them for their evil deeds.

Woe to them, for they have strayed from me. Disaster to
them, for they have rebelled against me. I would
redeem them but they have spoken falsely against me.

They have not called to me from their hearts. They howl on their beds and lacerate themselves for the local fertility gods, rebelling against me.

I have given cunning and strength to their arms and yet they contrive mischief against me. They turn to Báal and not to the Most High. They are like a long bow that has gone slack. Their princes shall fall by the sword because of the insolence of their tongues. They shall be the butt of Egyptian jokes.

8

Set the trumpet to your lips, for carrion birds swoop over the sanctuary of the Lord because Israel has broken my covenant and violated my laws.

Israel calls out to me for help, "My God, we acknowledge you!" But Israel has rejected the good, and their enemies shall pursue them.

They set up kings, but not by my will, and they make princes I never thought of. They have fashioned idols for themselves of silver and gold, and this shall cause their destruction.

I despise your calf-god, O Samaria. My anger is aroused by its idols. How long will it be before Israel returns to piety?

An artisan made it: it is not God. The calf of Samaria shall
   be shattered in pieces.

Israel has sown the wind and shall reap the whirlwind.
   There are no ears on the standing corn. The crop has
   no grain. And if there were grain, strangers would
   consume it as Israel is consumed. How shall they
   survive among the gentiles but as a worthless oddity?

Like a wild ass that has left the herd, it has run off alone,
   fleeing to Assyria. Ephraim consorts with gigolos.

They have temporized with other nations, but I will gather
   them up and remind them who they are, and they
   shall repent at what they have done, anointing kings
   and princes.

Ephraim has set up many altars but they have been altars to
   sin. I have instructed great things in my law but they
   rejected it as if it were irrelevant.

They sacrifice beasts for my offerings and they eat the flesh,
   but the Lord does not accept these offerings. Instead, I
   remember their iniquity and recall their sins. They
   shall go back to Egypt.

Israel has forgotten his maker and builds palaces. And
   Judah has many walled cities, but I will send a fire to
   his cities and it shall consume his fortresses.

9

Do not rejoice, O Israel. Do not exult like other people, for you have gone whoring, forsaking your God. You have had orgies on every threshing floor. Those threshing floors will produce no more grain and the winepresses shall fail.

They shall not live in the Lord's land. Ephraim shall go back to Egypt and eat unclean things in Assyria. They shall not make libations of wine before the Lord. These will not please him. Nor shall they bring him their sacrifices which shall be like the bread of mourners. All that eat of it shall be defiled for their bread shall be only to fend off hunger and shall not be acceptable in the house of the Lord.

What will you do on your festivals and at the feast days of the Lord? You have fled a crime scene, and Egypt receives you, and Memphis shall be your grave. The Nile will mourn for you.

Weeds shall inherit your land and thorns will grow in your courtyards. Israel shall know that the days of retribution have come.

Your great guilt has set your prophets to raving and your iniquities and hatred have driven your seers mad.

The prophet is the watchman of Ephraim, the people of
God. But you have set fowler's snares for your seers,
and there is hostility toward them in God's sanctuary.

You have corrupted yourselves as in the days of Saul at
Gibeah, and God will remember your sins and punish
you for your iniquities.

Like grapes in the desert, I found Israel. Your fathers were
the first fruits on the fig tree coming into season. But
they went to Báal-peor and gave themselves over to
shamefulness, and they became as detestable as what
they adored.

Ephraim's honor shall fly away like a bird, with no
childbirth, no gravid wombs, no conceptions. Even if
they rear children, I will bereave them and there shall
be none left.

Woe to them when I abandon them.

Ephraim's sons are destined to be prey to wild beasts. Give
them, O Lord . . . What? A womb that miscarries and
dry breasts.

Every wickedness there is, they committed in Gilgal, and
therefore I hate them. For their evil deeds, I will drive
them from my house and love them no longer. Their
princes are rebels.

Ephraim is ruined and their root is dried out. They shall
bear no fruit, and what issue they have, I will slay,
their darling children.

My God will cast them out, because they did not heed him.
They shall be wanderers among the gentiles.

10

Israel is a rank weed, and its fruit ripens. The more its fruit
grows, the more altars he builds and the more altars he
has, the richer his land becomes, and the better he
makes his sacrificial pillars.

But they are demented and they shall be condemned. The
Lord shall break down their altars and ruin their
images.

They may say, "We have no king and do not care, and we
do not fear the Lord." They have sworn falsely and
broken the covenant and judgment springs up like a
hemlock in the furrows of the field.

The inhabitants of Samaria fear the calf god of Beth-aven,
and the people mourn over it and the priests that
worshipped before it shall howl in the shame to which
its glory will turn.

It shall be carried to Assyria as a gift to the Great King, and
disgrace shall overwhelm Ephraim, and Israel shall be
mortified because of its disobedience.

Samaria and her king are swept away like refuse in the
harbor. The hill shrines of Aven are obliterated, those
shrines where Israel sinned. Thorns and thistles shall
grow over those altars that will beg the mountains,
Cover us, and entreat the hills, Fall on us.

Since the day of Gibeah, Israel has sinned, and there has
been no end to it. Shall not war overtake them in
Gibeah? I want to chastise them, and the nations shall
mass against them in hordes for their shameful deeds.

Ephraim is like a heifer that is broken to the yoke but
prefers to thresh corn. I will set it to plowing again.
Judah must plow and Jacob shall harrow. Sow justice
and reap what loyalty merits. Break up your fallow
ground and seek the Lord until he comes and rains
righteousness down upon you.

You have sown sin and reaped injustice. You have eaten
the fruit of lies. You trusted in your chariots and your
many soldiers, but the tumult of war shall rise against
you and your fortresses shall be ruined, as Shalman
despoiled Beth-arbel in the day of battle when
mothers were dashed to pieces upon their children's
corpses.

So it shall be done to you, Bethel, because of your great
wickedness. In the dawning of that day, the king of
Israel shall be utterly swept away.

II

When Israel was a child, I loved him and called him my
son, and took him out of Egypt. But the more I called
out to him, the more he turned away from my
prophets. He sacrificed to images of Báal and burned
incense before idols.

I taught Ephraim how to walk, taking him by the arms as a
parent does, but he did not think of me as their
protector.

I bound them to myself with cords of compassion and
bonds of love. I was kind to them as a farmer is kind
to his horses, taking their bits from their mouths and
feeding them.

But they will go back to slavery in Egypt or be subjects of
the king of Assyria, because they do not turn to me.
The sword shall slash over their cities and cut the bars
of their gates and destroy them in their fortresses, for
they are resolved on backsliding. They call upon new
gods as to the Most High, but they cannot help.

How can I abandon you, Ephraim? How can I surrender
you, Israel? How shall I ruin you as I ruined Admah,
or destroy you as I destroyed Zeboim? My heart is
wrung within me, and my compassion and rage fight
with each other.

I will not resolve in my anger on Ephraim's destruction. I
will not vent my fury, for I am God and not a man. I
am the Holy One in your midst, and I will not come
to ruin you.

They shall follow the Lord and he shall roar like a lion, and
when he roars, the children shall tremble in the west.
They shall come fluttering like birds from Egypt, and
flocking like doves from Assyria, and I will keep them
in their dovecotes.

But I am surrounded by the lies of Ephraim and the deceit
of the house of Israel, and Judah is still faithful to the
idols he worships.

12

Ephraim herds the wind. He chases the east wind all day
long. He makes a treaty with the duplicitous Assyrians
and carries tributes of oil to the violent Egyptians.

The Lord also has a complaint against Judah and will punish
Jacob according to his misconduct, requiting him for
his transgressions.

Even in the womb, Jacob took his brother Esau by the heel. In his manhood, he strove with God, wrestling with the angel and winning. He wept and made supplication. He met God at Bethel, and there God spoke with him, even the Lord God of hosts, whose name is the Lord, saying, Turn back to your God and persevere in love and justice, waiting continually on your God.

There are false scales in the merchant's hands and he loves to cheat. Ephraim says, "I have become rich, and have made my fortune," but his wealth cannot buy off his iniquity or reduce his guilt.

I am the Lord your God, from the land of Egypt, and I will make you live in tabernacles again as in the days of Succoth.

I spoke to the prophets and have multiplied their visions, and through the prophets have given parables.

Is there idolatry in Gilead? Surely it shall come to nothing. They sacrifice bullocks in Gilgal and heap their altars as thickly as furrows of the field.

Jacob fled to the land of Aram. Israel did service there for a wife, and for a wife he herded sheep. By a prophet the Lord brought Israel out of Egypt and by a prophet was Israel saved.

Ephraim has given bitter provocation, and the Lord shall
make him answerable for his bloodguilt and bring
down on his head the blame for what he has done.

13

When Ephraim spoke stammeringly, the prophet bore it for
Israel. But when Ephraim worshipped at Báal's altars,
the prophet died. And now they sin more and more,
and have cast images of silver and to idols, the work of
artisans, they say, "Sacrifice to these. Kiss the calves."

Therefore, they shall be like the morning mist that vanishes,
like chaff driven by the wind from the threshing floor,
or like smoke that rises from chimneys and disappears.

But I am the Lord your God and have been so since the
days of Egypt, and you shall have no God but me, for
beside me there is none who can save you.

I cared for you in the wilderness, in the heat of the deserts.
But when I brought you to the rich pasture lands, you
were filled and, being filled, you grew proud and your
hearts became haughty and you forgot me.

Therefore I will raven upon you like a lion, like a leopard
will I stalk you. I shall be a bear enraged by the loss of
its cubs and will rip you to the heart, and I will maul
you like a tiger, and like a wild beast I will rip you
apart.

O Israel, you have destroyed yourself. And who is there but
    me who can help you? I will be your king, for no
    other king can save you and protect your cities, and I
    will be your judge. You begged me for kings and
    princes. And I gave you a king but was offended, and I
    took your king away in my wrath.

Ephraim's guilt is inscribed in a scroll, and his sin is
    recorded.

When his mother went into labor with him, he showed
    himself an obstreperous child, for he did not present
    himself at the mouth of the womb when he was due.
    Shall I save him from the power of Sheol? Shall I
    redeem him from death?

Oh, for the plagues of Sheol and Oh, for the sting of Death!
    I will put compassion out of my sight.

Though he may flourish and be as numerous as the reeds,
    an east wind, the wind of the Lord, shall come from
    across the wilderness, and his fountains shall dry up
    and his springs shall be parched, and the wealth of his
    treasure shall blow away.

Samaria shall be desolate because she has rebelled against
    her God. Her children shall fall by the sword and be
    dashed to pieces and her pregnant women's bellies will
    be ripped open.

14

O Israel, return to the Lord your God, for you have
  stumbled because of your iniquity. Never mind the
  beasts you offered to Báal, but pray with words and
  beg God to cleanse you of your sins, and in his mercy
  receive you as you offer your tributes in words.

Assyria will not save us with its mighty cavalry. Idols we
  have made with our hands we shall no longer pray to
  as if they were gods. In you the orphan finds a parent's
  love.

I will heal their apostasy and I will love them freely, for my
  anger has turned away from them. I will be as the
  refreshing dew to Israel which shall blossom like the
  lily. His roots shall be as firm as the cedars of Lebanon.
  His branches shall spread and his beauty shall be as the
  fragrant olive groves of Lebanon.

Israel shall return to dwell in my shadow and shall flourish
  like a tended garden and blossom like a rich vineyard
  in Lebanon.

Ephraim shall say, "What do I want with idols?" I have
  heard him and I have seen him, and I am like an
  evergreen cypress, and from me comes his rich
  fruit.

Whoever is wise will understand these things and whoever is prudent shall know these things, for the ways of the Lord are righteous: the just shall walk in them, while the sinner shall stumble and fall.

JOEL

To Joel the son of Pethuel came these words of the Lord:

Listen, you elders, and all you who dwell in the land give
ear. Can you remember a thing like this? Have you
heard from your fathers talk of such a happening?

This is something we will speak of to our children and they
will tell their children and grandchildren.

In this catastrophe, what the grub has left, the larva has
eaten, and what the larva has not destroyed the pupa
has gnawed, and whatever they have overlooked, the
swarms of the adult locusts have devoured.

Even the drunkards have been roused from their dreams
and the tipplers have come out of their taverns to look
around, because there is no wine for them.

For a nation has come up against my people, a numberless
horde, and its teeth are like the teeth of a pitiless lion
and its fangs are those of a lioness.

It has wrecked my vines and splintered my fig tree, made it
bare and stripped its bark, and the trunk and branches
are white.

Lament, therefore, like a virgin who puts on sackcloth
instead of her bridal dress for the betrothed of her
heart.

There are no sacrifices at the temple, no meat offering and
grain offerings, no libations of olive oil or wine,
because there is nothing to offer. The field is empty
and the land mourns. There is no wine and no oil.

The farmers are ashamed and the vintners are mortified.
They howl together, for there is no wheat and no
barley. There are no harvests from the fields. The
vines are withered and the fig tree is barren. The
pomegranate, the apple, and the palm bear no fruit.
They are desolate as the sons of men are desolate.

Dress yourselves, then, in mourning, O priests, and lament.
Call the elders together in conclave and summon all
the inhabitants of the land into the house of the Lord,
and cry out.

Bewail the day!

The day of the Lord is at hand, and destruction will come
    from the Almighty.

Is not the good food gone? Are not joy and gladness gone
    from the house of God?

Under the clods of earth, the seed rots, and our storehouses
    are empty and our barns useless, for there is no grain.
    The beasts groan in their hunger. There is no
    pasturage for the cattle and nowhere for the sheep to
    graze.

To you, O Lord, I cry out, as the beasts cry to me,
    dismayed. For there is nothing, nothing: the field has
    been burned over and the trees are dead. The wild
    game is dying for their meadows are shriveled and
    their brooks have run dry.

2

Sound the ram's horn in Zion and raise the alarm on our
    holy mountain. Let all the inhabitants of the land
    tremble, for the day of the Lord is at hand, a dark and
    ominous day, with clouds thick in the morning that
    overwhelm the mountains.

A great and powerful army comes swarming over these
mountains. There has never been anything like it, and
never shall there be anything like it again, even
through all the generations.

They are like a fire that devours as it goes. Before them is
an Eden and behind them is a desolation, a wasteland.
Nothing escapes them.

They are like horsemen, leaping and running. They come
with a rattle of chariots and the crackle of fire that
clears away stubble. They are martial minions drawn
up for war.

Before their implacable faces, the people shall be appalled
and woeful. They shall come running, swarming like
infantry and climbing the walls, each marching in
rank, relentless and unstoppable as they move forward
in their dreadful good order. And no weapon will
deter them, but they shall keep coming and coming.

They shall overwhelm the city's walls and run through the
streets, and they shall break into the houses, entering
through the windows like thieves.

The earth trembles before them, and the heavens shake.
The sun and the moon are dark, and the stars are no
longer visible.

The Lord calls out to his army, for his troops are
    numberless and he is strong.

As they carry out his orders, the day of the Lord is terrible,
    terrible and who can expect to endure it?

But even now, the Lord says, Return to me, come back
    with your heart, with fasting, weeping, and mourning
    and with prayers of repentance, and instead of tearing
    your garments, tear your very hearts in contrition.

For who can be sure that it is too late to turn and repent, to
    leave a blessing behind you, and to offer grain and
    meat and wine to the Lord your God?

Sound the shofar and sanctify the fast. Call a solemn
    assembly and gather the people in conclave. Bless the
    congregation and call the elders together. Gather the
    children, even the nursing infants, and let the
    bridegroom leave his new house and the bride her
    nuptial chamber.

Between the porch and the altar let the priests weep who
    are the ministers of the Lord, and let them implore,
    "Spare your people O Lord, and do not make your
    heritage a reproach among nations." Among the
    nations, consider how they will ask: "Where is their
    God?"

Then will the Lord care for his land and pity his people.

Yes, and the Lord will answer his people's prayers and say,
Behold, I will send you grain and wine and oil, and
you shall be satisfied. And I will no longer let you be
mocked among the heathen.

I will drive off the invading army, harry him into a desolate
land with his face to the Mediterranean and his rear to
the Dead Sea, and a vile stench will arise from his
corpses, for his crimes have been enormous.

Do not despair, O land, for the Lord, too, is enormous and
will do great things. Do not fear, you beasts of the
field, for the grasses will grow in the wilderness, and
the trees will bear fruit. The vine will bear again, and
the fig tree will yield again.

Be glad you children of Zion and rejoice in the Lord, your
God, for he has brought the rain in October for
planting and in March for the mature crops, and the
rains will come as they used to do.

And the threshing floors will be full of wheat again, and the
vats shall be full to overflowing of wine and oil. And
what the nymph and the pupa and the larva and the
mature locust in the army I sent have eaten, I shall
restore to you.

And you will eat and have plenty and be satisfied and praise
the name of the Lord who has dealt with you
wonderfully well, and my people shall not be ashamed.

You shall know that I am in the midst of Israel, and that I
am the Lord your God, and none other. And never
again shall my people be put to shame.

It will happen that I shall pour out my spirit on your flesh
like rain, and your sons and your daughters shall
prophecy, and your old men dream dreams and your
young men see visions, and even upon the servants
shall I pour out my spirit and make them believe.

I will show wonders in the sky and on the earth, blood and
fire and pillars of smoke. The sun shall go dark and the
moon will be blood red to announce that the great and
terrible day of the Lord is at hand.

And in that time, whoever shall call on the name of the
Lord shall be saved, and on Mount Zion and in
Jerusalem there shall be deliverance, as the Lord has
promised, and those whom the Lord has called shall be
among the survivors.

3

For you will see in those days, I shall restore the fortunes of
Judah and Jerusalem. I will gather all the nations and
bring them to the valley of Jehoshaphat, the valley of
judgment, and I will plead there for my people and for
Israel, my heritage, because they have scattered them
among the nations and have divided my land.

They have cast lots for my people and have given a boy's
life for a whore and have sold a girl for wine they have
drunk.

What are you to me, O Tyre and Sidon? What are you,
Philistia, along the coast? Do you pay me back for
some wrong or slight? If you exact recompense from
me, I shall requite your wickedness speedily and it will
be on your head.

You have taken my silver and gold and carried away into
your temples my sacred objects. The children of Judah
and of Israel you sold as slaves to the Greeks to clear
them from the land.

But behold, I will raise them up from where you have sold
them and will pay you back. I will sell your sons and
daughters to the children of Judah, and they shall resell
them to Sheba, far off in Arabia. Thus has the Lord
pronounced:

Let it be proclaimed among the gentiles to prepare for war
and to let their soldiers come together. Let them all
assemble.

Beat your plowshares into swords and your pruning hooks
into spears, but it will do no good, for the weak will
admit that I am the strong one.

Muster yourselves, you heathen, gather yourselves together
and arm yourselves. Try what you will.

Let all the pagans rouse themselves and march into the
valley of Jehoshaphat, for there I will sit and judge all
the heathens of every quarter.

Whet the sickle, for the harvest is ripe. Come all of you,
tread, for the press is full and the vats overflow: their
wickedness is abundant.

The multitudes, the multitudes are in the valley of
judgment, for the day of the Lord is at hand there in
the valley of judgment.

The sun shall go dark and the moon, and the stars shall hide
their shining as the Lord roars from Zion and the
sound of his voice goes forth from Jerusalem and the
heavens shake and the earth trembles.

But to his people, the Lord is a refuge and a stronghold.
Know that I am your God dwelling in Zion my holy
mountain. Jerusalem shall be holy and there shall be no
strangers passing through her gates anymore.

It shall come to pass in that day that the mountains shall
drop down sweet wine and the hills shall flow with
milk, and all the stream beds of Judah shall flow with
water. A fountain shall come forth from the house of
the Lord to bring water to the valley of Shittim where
the acacias grow.

Egypt shall be a desert and Edom shall be a wilderness for
their violence against the children of Judah, because
they have shed innocent blood in their land. But Judah
shall dwell for ever and Jerusalem shall endure from
generation to generation.

I shall avenge their blood and will not excuse the guilty, for
the Lord lives in Zion.

AMOS

The words of Amos, a sheep rancher of Tekoa, that came
to him about Israel in the days of Uzziah king of Judah
and of Jeraboam, the son of Joash, king of Israel, two
years before the earthquake:

He said, The Lord roars from Zion and raises his voice
from Jerusalem. The pastures of the shepherds droop
and the top of Mount Carmel parches.

Thus says the Lord: For three transgressions of Damascus
and for four, I will complete their punishment, for
they have whipped Gilead with threshers of iron. I
will therefore send a fire to destroy the house of
Hazael and it shall raze the forts of Benhadad.

I will break the gate of Damascus and cut off the inhabitant
in the Valley of Aven and him who holds the scepter
of the house of Eden, says the Lord, and the people of
Syria shall go into exile to Kir.

Thus says the Lord: For three transgressions of Gaza and for
four, I will complete their punishment, because they
carried an entire people into exile and delivered them
to the Edomites. I will therefore send a fire to destroy
the wall of Gaza and it shall raze her forts. I will cut off
the inhabitants from Ashdod and him that holds the
scepter in Ashkelon. I will turn my hand against
Ekron, the Lord God says, and the remnant of the
Philistines shall perish.

Thus says the Lord: For three transgressions of Tyre and for
four, I will complete their punishment, because they
delivered an entire people to Edom and did not
remember their fraternal covenant. I will therefore
send a fire upon the wall of Tyre and it shall raze her
forts.

Thus says the Lord: For three transgressions of Edom and
for four, I will complete the punishment, because he
pursued his brother with the sword and thrust out all
pity from his heart, and his anger gnawed at him
perpetually and he kept his rage alive forever. So I will
send a fire upon Teman and it shall raze his forts at
Bozrah.

Thus says the Lord: For three transgressions of the
    Ammonites and for four, I will complete the
    punishment, because they have raped and killed
    pregnant women in Gilead in their expansionist wars.
    I will set fire to the walls of Rabbah and it shall raze
    their forts. There will be shouting on the day of battle,
    and a tempest like a tornado on that day, says the
    Lord, and their king shall go into exile with his princes
    and courtiers.

2

Thus says the Lord: For three transgressions of Moab and
    for four, I will complete the punishment, because he
    burned the bones of the king of Edom in his lime pits.
    I will send a fire upon Moab and it shall raze the forts
    of Kirioth, and Moab shall die with screams and
    groans and the blare of the trumpets.

I will cut down the ruler from their midst, says the Lord,
    and slay their princes with him.

And thus says the Lord: For three transgressions of Judah
    and for four, I will complete the punishment, because
    they have despised the Lord's law and have failed to
    keep his commandments, and their lies have led them
    astray in the way their fathers went astray. I will send a
    fire upon Judah and it shall raze the forts of Jerusalem.

And thus says the Lord: For three transgressions of Israel
and for four, I will complete the punishment, because
they have betrayed the righteous for silver and sold the
poor into slavery for a pair of shoes.

They trample the faces of the poor into the dust and turn
aside from the afflicted. A man and his father go to the
same whore and they profane my holy name.

They come to pray at my altar sporting the pawned
clothing of the poor, and in the temple they drink the
wine of those whose goods have been repossessed.

I destroyed the mighty Amorites who were haughty as
cedars and strong as oak trees. I destroyed his fruit
above and his roots in the earth. And I brought you
from the land of Egypt and led you for forty years
through the desert to possess the land of the Amorites.

I raised up your sons to be prophets and your youths to be
consecrated Nazirites, O children of Israel, asks the
Lord, is it not true?

But you offered the Nazirites wine and tempted them, and
you commanded the prophets not to prophesy.

I will weigh you down as a cart is weighed down when it is
full of sheaves. The swift shall no longer be fleet of
foot and the strong shall become weak, and the mighty
shall be helpless to save his life. The bowman shall run
away, and the infantryman shall flee but not fast
enough, nor will the cavalryman be able to escape.
Your brave soldiers shall throw away their armor and
flee naked from the field. Thus says the Lord.

3

Hear this word that the Lord has spoken against you, O
children of Israel, against all of you whom I brought
out of the land of Egypt:

You alone have I known of all the peoples of the earth.
Therefore I will punish you all the more severely for
your iniquities.

Can two walk together unless they agree on the way they
are going?

Will a lion roar in the forest when he has no prey? Will a
lion cub growl in his den if he has nothing to eat?

Will a bird be trapped in a snare where there is no bait for
it? And shall the fowler take up a snare that has no bird
in it?

Shall the trumpet be blown in the city and the people not
be afraid? And shall evil befall a city without the Lord
having caused it?

Surely, the Lord God does nothing without revealing his
secrets to the prophets, his servants.

The lion has roared. Who is not afraid? The Lord God has
spoken. Who can not prophesy?

Proclaim it to the strongholds of Assyria and to the
fortresses in Egypt, and say, Muster yourselves in the
mountains of Samaria, and see the great tumults there
and the oppressions in her midst.

For they have no idea how to do right, says the Lord, and
they store up the take of their violence and theft in
their palaces. Therefore, says the Lord God, an
adversary shall come to their borders and bring down
their defenses, and their strongholds shall be
plundered.

The Lord says, As the shepherd takes from the mouth of the
lion a leg or a piece of an ear, so shall the children of
Israel be taken out who dwell in Samaria on the
corner of a bed or on a pallet in Damascus.

Listen and testify in the house of Jacob, says the Lord God,
the God of hosts. In that day I shall punish the
transgressions of Israel and demolish the altars of
Bethel, and the horns of the altar shall be destroyed
and shall fall to the ground. And I will smite the
winter palace and the summer palace and the houses of
ivory shall be destroyed and the sumptuary villas shall
come to an end.

4

Hear this word up in the mountains of Samaria, you cows
of Bashan. You oppress the poor and crush the
indigent, and say to your masters, Fetch me my drink!
The Lord God has sworn by his very holiness that the
days are coming when they shall take away your
corpses with great hooks and your children's corpses
with gaffers.

You shall go out through the gaps in your city's walls and
led like cattle you shall be cast forth naked into
ditches.

Come, then to Bethel, and sin. And at Gilgal compound
your sins. Bring your sacrifices every morning and your
tithes every third day. Offer your sacrifices of
thanksgiving with leavened bread and announce to
everyone your generous freewill offerings the way you
love to do, O people of Israel. Thus says the Lord God.

I stripped your cities bone clean, and there was not a crumb
in any of your palaces, but you have not returned to
me, says the Lord. I withheld the rain from you when
there were three months to go before the harvest, or I
made it rain on one city but not on another, or made
it rain on one field and not on another in which the
crops withered. And fugitives from two or three cities
journeyed into another town that still had water, but
they were not satisfied. And still you have not returned
to me, says the Lord.

I have afflicted you with blight and mildew. I have laid
your gardens and vineyards waste. Locusts have
devoured your fig trees and your olive trees, and still
you did not return to me, says the Lord.

I have sent plagues upon you the way I sent plagues to
Egypt. I have slain your young men with the sword,
and I have rustled your horses, and made the stink of
your camp arise in your nostrils, and still you did not
return to me, says the Lord.

I overthrew some of you as when I destroyed Sodom and
Gomorra, and the rest of you were like a brand
plucked out of the fire, and still you did not return to
me, says the Lord.

Therefore I will do to you what I threaten, and because I
will do this, O Israel, you should prepare to meet your
God.

For, see, he who made the mountains and created the wind
and declared to man what his thought was and lifts the
morning's darkness and walks upon the heights of the
earth, the Lord, the God of hosts is his name.

5

Hear this word that I speak against you, my lamentation, O
house of Israel:

The virgin Israel is fallen and shall not rise again. She is
forsaken in her land and there is no one to raise her up.

For this is what the Lord God says: The city that sent out a
thousand troops shall have only a hundred left, and
that which sent out a hundred shall leave only ten to
the house of Israel.

For the Lord says to the house of Israel: Only by trusting in
me shall you live.

Do not bet on Bethel or expect much at all from Gilgal. Of
Beersheba out there in the desert, despair. Gilgal shall
fall and Bethel as well.

Seek the Lord and you shall live, for he breaks out like a
purging fire in the house of Joseph. He consumes the
house and no one of you in Bethel can extinguish
him. Your judgment turns to bitter wormwood and
you cast righteousness down into the dirt.

Seek him who made the Pleiades and Orion and who turns
the shadow of death into the light of dawn and then
brings the day to its dusk, who calls forth the waters of
the sea and pours them on the face of the earth. The
Lord is his name.

He brings destruction to the mighty and ruins proud
fortresses.

You mistreat those who stand at the palace gates to protest
and who speak the truth in the marketplace. You
trample the poor man and take from his store of
wheat. You have your villas of hewn stone but you
shall not live in them, and your pleasant hillside
vineyards, but you shall not drink their wine, for I
know how many are your sins and how grievous are
your faults.

You harass the righteous and you solicit bribes and you
turn aside from the needy at your gate. And everyone
knows this, but these are bad times and the prudent
keep silent.

Seek good and not evil, so that you may live and the Lord,
the God of hosts, shall be with you, as you say in your
prayers.

Loathe evil and love good, and establish justice at your
palace gates. Then the Lord God of hosts may show
his grace and his judgment to the remnant of Joseph.

The Lord, the God of hosts, says, There shall be wailing in
the city squares and on all the highways they shall cry
out, Woe! woe! And they shall call the farmer to
mourning and those who are skilled in lamentation
they shall summon to wail. And in the vineyards there
shall be crying, the Lord says, as I come through
among you.

Take care, all you who desire the day of the Lord, for how
can you know what it will mean? The day of the Lord
brings darkness and not light. A man flees from a lion
but he encounters a bear. Or he flees for safety into his
house where he leans his hand on the wall but there a
viper bites him.

Is not the day of the Lord's judgment darkness and not
light? Black, black, and with no glimmer of brightness
in it!

I hate your feasts, and I will have nothing to do with your
prayer meetings. You offer me burnt offerings and
flesh on the altar, but I disdain them. Neither will I
accept the peace offerings of your fatted beasts. I do
not want the racket of your singing. I will not listen to
the twangle of your instruments.

Instead, let justice roll down like a river, and righteousness
flow like a mighty stream.

Did you bring me sacrifices during your forty years in the
wilderness, O house of Israel?

But now you take up your idols and your icons, your
Sakkuth and Kaiwan, the images you have made? For
that reason, I will send you into captivity, far away
beyond Damascus, says the Lord whose name is the
God of hosts.

6

Woe to them who are at ease in Zion and who feel secure in
the mountain of Samaria, the chiefs and the potentates
to whom the house of Israel comes for their opinions.

Pass over to Calneh and look, or go to the great Hamath.
Can your chiefs compare with the rulers of those
kingdoms? Is your territory better than theirs?

You deny that the evil day is coming, even as you invite its
violence to approach.

Woe to those who lie upon beds of ivory and stretch out
on their rich couches, eating the dainty lambs from the
flock and the succulent calves from the barns, who
chant to the sound of the harp and sing pretty songs,
inventing new musical figures as if they were Davids
and drinking wine from handsome bowls and
anointing themselves with expensive oils. They do not
grieve for the ruin of Joseph!

Therefore they shall be the first of the captives who go into exile and the revelry of their banquets shall die away in their ears. The Lord God has sworn by his own holiness, and the Lord, the God of hosts, says, I hate the arrogance of Jacob and detest his palaces and therefore I will deliver up his city and everything in it.

If ten men take refuge together in a house during the siege, they shall die of the pestilence. And someone's kinsman shall come along to burn the corpses and bring the bones out of the house, and he shall ask a neighbor if anyone is still alive inside. And the neighbor shall say, No, and not mention that the Lord is inside, for at such a time we may not mention the name of the Lord.

It is the Lord's will, that the earthquake will come and the great house shall be shattered into fragments and the cottage be dashed into bits.

Do horses run on the rocks? Does the plowman plow the sea with oxen? You have turned judgment into gall and righteousness into bitter wormwood. You rejoice in your victory at Lo-debar and exult in your triumph, taking Ashteroth-karnaim. But watch, I will raise up a nation against you, O house of Israel, says the Lord, the God of hosts, and they shall oppress you from Lebanon in the north to the farthest border of the south.

7

This is the vision the Lord God gave me: There he was making a swarm of locusts, when the spring rains were bringing the crops along, and it was time for the harvest of the first yield, and the locusts were about to devour everything in the fields, and I said, O Lord God, have mercy, I beg you. How can Jacob stand this? He is so weak! And the Lord relented and said, It shall not be.

And the Lord God showed me another vision, and, see, the Lord called for a judgment by fire, and it devoured the ocean and was about to consume the land, and I said, O Lord God, I beg you! How can Jacob stand this? He is so weak! And the Lord relented and said, It shall not be.

And the Lord God showed me another vision, and, see, the Lord was standing next to a wall built with a plumb line, with the plumb line in his hand, and the Lord said, Amos what do you see? And I said, A plumb line. And the Lord said, Watch, I am setting the plumb line amidst my people Israel. I will not ignore them anymore.

The high places of Isaac shall be turned desolate, and the sanctuaries of Israel shall be laid waste. I will rise against the house of Jeroboam with the sword.

Then Amaziah, the priest of Bethel, sent to Jeroboam king of Israel, saying, "Amos conspires against you in the midst of the house of Israel. The nation cannot endure all his words. For Amos says that Jeroboam shall die by the sword and Israel shall be driven into exile from their own land."

And Amaziah said to Amos, "O prophet, run away into the land of Judah, and earn your bread there and prophesy there, but do not stay here and prophesy at Bethel, for it is the king's sanctuary and it is the king's court."

Then Amos answered, "I am no prophet or the son of a prophet, but just a sheep rancher and a cultivator of sycamore trees. But the Lord took me as I was following my flock and the Lord said to me, Go and prophesy to my people Israel."

Therefore, hear the word of the Lord. You say not to prophesy against Israel or preach against the house of Isaac. But the Lord says, Your wife shall be a whore on the city streets and your sons and daughters shall die by the sword, and your lands shall be parcelled out and sold, and you shall die in an unclean place, and all Israel shall surely go into exile far from its homeland.

8

This is the vision the Lord showed me: Behold, a basket of
summer fruit. And he said, Amos, what do you see?
And I said, A basket of summer fruit. And the Lord
said to me, The end is come to my people Israel. I will
not ignore them anymore.

The songs of the temple shall be howlings in that day, said
the Lord God, and there shall be corpses everywhere,
and they shall heap them up in silence.

You who trample on the needy and oppress the poor of the
land, hear this. You ask when the celebration of the
new moon will be over so you can sell corn, and when
the Sabbath will be ended so you may sell wheat,
scanting your measures, inflating your prices, and
cooking your books by trickery, so that you can
foreclose on the poor and repossess even the shoes of
the needy as you deal in spoiled wheat.

The Lord has sworn by the holiness of Jacob, Surely I will
not forget any of their misdeeds. Shall the land not
tremble for this, and shall not its inhabitants mourn?
My anger shall rise up like a flood and it shall drown
everything as the Nile does in Egypt.

And it shall happen on that day, says the Lord God, that I
will make the sun go down at noon and darken the
earth in the middle of the day. I will turn your feasts
into mourning and your songs into lamentations and
you will wear sackcloth on your bodies and shave your
heads, and I will make it as if you were mourning
your only son and I will make the end of it a bitter
day.

See, the day will come, says the Lord God, when I will
send a famine onto the land, not a famine of bread or a
thirst for water, but a hunger for the words of the
Lord. And people shall wander from sea to sea and
from the north to the east, and they shall run this way
and that seeking the word of the Lord, and not find it.
In that day, shall the beautiful virgins and the strong
young men faint in their thirst.

They who swear by Ashimah in Samaria and take oaths by
the local gods of Dan and Beersheba shall be destroyed
and never rise again.

9

I saw the Lord standing beside the altar, and he said, Strike
the capitals of the doors so that the posts may shake and
shatter them on the heads of the people. And whoever
remains alive, I will slay with the sword so that not one
of them shall escape and not one shall survive.

Let them dig down to Sheol, but my hand will find them.
Let them climb up even to heaven, but I will grab
them and bring them down. Let them hide themselves
on the top of mount Carmel, but I will seek them out.
Let them be hidden from my sight at the bottom of
the sea, but I will find a serpent and send it to bite
them.

And if they go into captivity before their enemies, I will
still oppress them with the sword and it shall slay
them, and I will keep my eye on them for evil and not
for good.

The Lord God of hosts is he who touches the earth and it
melts and all who dwell in it mourn. His anger rises up
like the Nile, but it sinks back again, like the Nile of
Egypt.

He builds his upper chambers in the heavens and establishes
his vaults on the earth. He calls for the waters of the
sea and pours them out on the face of the earth. The
Lord is his name.

Are you not as foreign to me as the Ethiopians, O children
of Israel? Have I not brought Israel out of the land of
Egypt, the Lord asks, and saved Israel from the
Philistines from Caphtor and the Syrians from Kir?

Behold, the eyes of the Lord God are on the sinful
kingdom. And I will destroy it from the face of the
earth, except that I will not utterly obliterate the house
of Jacob, says the Lord.

For I will command that the house of Israel be sifted among
the nations as corn is sifted in a sieve, but the least
grain shall not fall upon the earth. All the sinners of
my people who think evil shall not overtake them shall
die by the sword.

In that day, I will raise up the fallen tabernacle of David
and repair its gaps, restore its ruins, and rebuild it as in
the days of old, and Israel shall again possess what is
left in the land of Edom, and all the nations David
conquered shall be restored to you. Thus says the
Lord, who will do this.

Behold, in the days to come, the Lord says, the plowman
and the harvester shall jostle one another, and the
treader of grapes and the sower of seed shall meet in
their labor, and the mountains shall drip sweet wine
and the hills shall flow with it.

I will restore the fortunes of my people Israel and they shall
rebuild their ruined cities and inhabit them. They shall
plant vineyards and drink their wine, and they shall
make gardens and eat their fruit. And I will plant them
upon their land and they shall never again be uprooted
from the land that I have given them. Thus says the
Lord your God.

OBADIAH

The vision of Obadiah, servant of God:

The Lord God says this about Edom. He has sent his
   messenger among the nations with this word: "Rise
   up, let us rise against Edom in battle."

I have said to Edom, I will make you small among the
   nations. You will be altogether despised. You have
   been proud of heart, but you have deceived
   yourselves. Because you live in steep rocky passes, you
   imagine yourselves lofty and grand. You say to
   yourselves, "Who will bring us down to the ground?"

Though you soar like an eagle and your nest is as high as
   the stars, I will bring you down, says the Lord.

If thieves came to you, if robbers came by night, they
would steal only what they could carry. If vagrants
came to pilfer your vines, they would still leave you
some of the grapes. But how absolutely will the land
of Esau be pillaged! Your treasure will be all gone.

All your allies will betray you. They will drive you from
your borders. The friends you trust will combine
against you to ensnare you. It beggars the mind. The
wise men of Edom I will destroy on that day, the Lord
says. On Mount Esau there will be no more
temporizing and explanation.

The mighty men of the city of Teman shall be dismayed,
cut off from Mount Esau and slaughtered. For your
violence against your brother Jacob, shame shall cover
you and you shall be rejected forever.

At the critical moment, when the strangers came to take us
away as captive, when foreigners entered into our
gates and divided up Jerusalem's plunder, you were
one of them and were with them.

You should have been there like a brother, but you were a
stranger. You should not have rejoiced at Judah's ruin.
You should not have gloated on the day of our
downfall.

On the day of my people's calamity, you should not have
   entered into our gates to look on, exult, and loot our
   goods.

You should not have stood at the crossroads to cut off our
   fugitives and deliver up our survivors in that time of
   our pain.

For the day of the Lord is near, coming to all the gentiles,
   and as you have done so shall it be done to you. Your
   deeds shall come back and be on your own head.

As you have drunk on our holy mountain, so shall the
   nations drink you down and swallow you up until
   they stagger. It shall be as though you had never been.

But on Mount Zion shall be deliverance and holiness and
   the house of Jacob shall regain its possessions.

Jacob shall be a fire, and Joseph will be a flame, and Esau
   will be the stubble they devour. There shall be
   nothing left of the house of Esau, for the Lord has
   decreed it.

The Israelites of the Negev shall possess the mount of Esau,
   and those of the lowlands of Sephelah will drive out
   the Philistines on the coast. Israel will possess again the
   fields of Ephraim and Samaria, and the tribe of
   Benjamin shall have Gilead.

And the exiles of the Northern Kingdom shall occupy the
land of Canaan, even as far north as Zarephath. And
the exiles from Jerusalem shall come back from Sardis
and shall have the cities of the Negev.

The saviors of Israel shall ascend Mount Zion again and we
shall rule Mount Esau, and the kingdom shall be
restored according to the will of the Lord.

JONAH

The word of the Lord came to Jonah, the son of Amittai,
saying, Arise and go to Nineveh, that great city, and
cry out against it, for their wickedness offends me.

But Jonah fled the Lord and ran away to Tarshish. He went
to Joppa and found a ship bound for Tarshish and paid
the fare and boarded, thinking to get away from the
Lord's country and find refuge in Tarshish.

But the Lord sent forth a great wind onto the ocean so that
it seemed the ship would break up. The sailors were
afraid and each man prayed to his god and they threw
the cargo overboard to lighten the vessel, but Jonah
had gone below decks and he lay fast asleep.

The captain found him there and asked what he thought he was doing. Arise, you sluggard, and call on your god. Perhaps your god will listen to you and keep us all from drowning.

The sailors agreed that they would cast lots to know who was the evil one who had brought this catastrophe upon them. They cast lots and Jonah drew the short straw. So they asked him, "What is this evil you have done? What is your occupation and where do you come from? Who are your people? Who are you?"

He answered, "I am a Hebrew and I fear the Lord, the God of heaven, who made the sea and the dry land." And he told them that he had fled from the Lord, and they were afraid and they asked him why he had done this.

But one of the sailors said the real question was what to do now to Jonah that would calm the sea, for the waves were huge and the wind was howling.

Jonah said to them, "Throw me overboard, and the sea will be calmed, because I know that it is because of me that this storm has come upon you."

But the sailors rowed hard to try to make land, but they could not for the sea heaved terribly and the storm tossed them cruelly. So they cried to the Lord, "We beg you, O God, let us not die for this man's sake. Do not take our innocent blood. We will do what you want."

And therefore they took Jonah and threw him into the sea, and the water was calmed and it raged no more. And the men were awestruck and offered a sacrifice to the Lord and thanked him.

Now God had prepared a great fish and it appeared and swallowed Jonah up, and Jonah was in the belly of the fish for three days and nights.

2

And from the belly of the fish, Jonah prayed to the Lord, his God.

He described it later, saying, I called out in my trouble to the Lord and he heard me. I cried out as from the belly of Sheol and you heard my voice. For you were the one who threw me into the sea, and the waves broke all around me and the water covered my head, and I said, I am cast out of your sight and I will look again to your holy temple.

The waters overwhelmed me. My soul was drowning. The depths had me in their clutches and the seaweed was wrapped around my head. I was at the very floor of the sea, the earth's foundation, trapped, buried alive, and you, O Lord, my God, you rescued me as you would retrieve one from the grave.

My soul had fainted within me, but I remembered the
   Lord, and my prayer reached you and arrived at your
   holy temple. Those who trust in themselves give up
   their chance for your mercy.

But I will sacrifice to you. With the voice of thanksgiving,
   I will fulfill my promises, for deliverance comes from
   the Lord.

And the Lord commanded the fish, and it vomited Jonah
   out onto the dry land.

3

The word of the Lord came to Jonah a second time, saying,
   Get up and go to Nineveh that great city, and preach
   to it the message I have given you. So Jonah got up
   and went to Nineveh as the Lord had told him to do.

Nineveh was a very great city, seventy five miles across.
   And Jonah went there and crossed through it, calling
   out, "In forty days, Nineveh shall be destroyed."

The people of Nineveh believed God and proclaimed a fast
   and they put on sackcloth, from the greatest of them
   down to the least. Even the king of Nineveh, when he
   heard the news, got down from his throne and laid his
   robe aside and put on sackcloth and sat in ashes.

He caused it to be proclaimed throughout Nineveh by
 decree of the king and his council that all should fast,
 and that neither man nor beast, herd of cattle nor flock
 of sheep should taste anything, neither food nor drink.
 But let man and beast be covered with sackcloth and
 cry aloud to God. Let each of them turn from his evil
 ways and from the violence that his hands have done.

Who can tell if God may relent and turn away his terrible
 anger so that we do not perish?

And God saw what they did and how they had turned away
 from their evil practices, and he relented. What he had
 said he would do to them, he did not do. And this
 displeased Jonah very much and made him angry.

4

He prayed to the Lord and said, Lord, this is why I fled to
 Tarshish. You are a gracious god, and merciful, and
 slow to anger, and of much loving kindness, and you
 relent in your anger.

I beg you, then, take my life from me, because I am
 ashamed, and it is better for me to die than to live.

But the Lord said, Is it right for you to be angry?

Jonah left the city and went to the countryside to the east, and there he set up a lean-to and sat under it in the shade, waiting to see what would happen to the city. And the Lord God made a vine that grew up over Jonah to give him shade and to deliver him from his anguish. And Jonah was grateful for the gourd.

But the next day, God created a worm, and then at dawn the worm attacked the vine and it withered and died. And when the sun rose, God made a hot simoom to blow on Jonah while the sun beat down on his head, and he fainted and could not bear it, and he said, It is better for me to die than to live.

And God said to Jonah, Is it right for you to be angry about the gourd? And Jonah answered, I am right to be angry, even to death.

And the Lord said, You had pity for the gourd for which you did not labor and which you did not plant and make grow. It came up in a night and it died in a night. And should I not spare Nineveh, that great city, where there are more than a hundred and twenty thousand people, innocent as children who do not know their right hand from their left, as dumb as their cows?

MICAH

The word of the Lord that came to Micah of Moresheth in the days of Jotham, Ahaz, and Hezekiah, kings of Judah. These are the visions he had about Samaria and Jerusalem.

Listen, all you people. Everyone on earth, pay heed, for the Lord God testifies against you, the Lord from his holy temple. He comes forth from his dwelling place and descends to walk on the high places of the earth.

The mountains will melt under him like wax in a fire and split apart to make valleys in which waters will cascade.

Why? Because of the transgressions of Jacob and for the sins of the house of Israel! Look at Samaria and the corruption of Jacob. Look at Jerusalem and the corruption of the house of Judah.

See how the Lord reduced Samaria to rubble, to a bare hill where you could plant a vineyard. The stones of their buildings are knocked down into the valley and you can see the gaping holes of the foundations.

Therefore will I cry and wail. I shall strip myself and go naked, howling like the jackals and screaming like the ostriches for what has happened to Judah.

Jerusalem's wound is incurable. There is no hope. And destruction is at the gates of my people.

The Assyrians are coming. Do not be aghast at what happened in Gath or worry about them. Do not bewail Beth-leaphrah or roll in the dust for their sakes. Do not be sad about Saphir and its naked shame.

Do the inhabitants of Zaanan groan on? Is Beth-ezel not doing well? At Maroth are they waxing wroth? Evil has come down from the Lord and it approaches the gates of Jerusalem!

What do they wish, the sinners of Lachish? To harness their
 speedy horses and get away in their chariots? You
 were the hotbed of sin, and from you came the
 corruption that has reached Jerusalem.

You are running for your lives and saying good-by to
 Moresheth-gath. Achzib shall be a delusion to the
 kings of Israel.

Ruin shall come to Mareshah and the glory of Israel shall
 vanish in a new Adullam.

Tear out your hair and weep for your sweet children. Make
 yourselves bald as an eagle, for they will take flight
 into captivity.

2

Woe to them who lie in bed scheming to work evil and
 contrive wickedness and, when the morning comes,
 act upon their schemes because they can.

When they want a man's field, they take it by violence, or a
 man's house, and they harry him and oppress him and
 rob him of his inheritance.

Therefore, the Lord says: Watch, I will bring evil to this
 family from which there will be no escape. You will
 bow your heads and not go haughtily, for you will
 know what oppression can be.

You will be the subject of jokes and of sad songs. And men shall sing how you have been utterly ruined and the dispossessors have been dispossessed. What you have done to your neighbors, the Assyrians shall do to you, dividing up your fields among themselves.

This will happen to the congregation of the Lord. I prophesy, but you will not listen. I indict you, but you have no shame.

But must not such things be said? You are the house of Jacob and should know that the spirit of the Lord is not to be constrained. To the righteous man who will listen, my words will sound good.

You have risen up against one another as though against an enemy. You strip the robes from the backs of peaceful men. The widows and orphans of my people you evict from the refuge of their houses. You turn little children out into the streets and you sully my glory forever.

This is a call to arms. There must be a war against the pollution that shall otherwise destroy you and bring you to ruin.

You prefer your false prophets? They assure you that you are right to swill wine and be comfortable. Those are the prophets you want to hear but they are lying to you.

3

I said to them, Listen, you chiefs of Jacob and you princes
of the house of Israel. Are you not supposed to know
right from wrong?

But you hate the good and you love wickedness. You tear
the very skin off your people and you pluck the flesh
from their bones.

You flay my people alive and raven on their flesh, breaking
their bones and cutting them up for your stewpot on
the fire.

You pray to God, do you? But he will not hear you. He
will hide his face from you because you have behaved
wretchedly and done wicked deeds.

You have your prophets but they condone what you do,
and the Lord hates them for leading you astray. They
are peaceful as lambs when you have bought them off
and militant against evil only if they are hungry.

It is a dark day when you listen to them, a day like night,
and you grope in the dark without a glimmer
anywhere. The sun shall set upon those prophets and
the day shall be black as night over them. Those seers
shall be ashamed and those soothsayers confounded.
They shall cover their mouths for no word of God is
in them.

I am the one with the power and the spirit of the Lord. I
am the one with justice and the strength to declare to
Jacob what his wickedness has been, and to Israel how
he has sinned.

Listen to me, you officials of the house of Jacob and you
leaders of the house of Israel who have made crooked
what once was straight and who hate justice. You are
building Zion on blood and the foundation of your
Jerusalem is iniquity.

The judges take bribes and the priests make rulings for
money. The prophets pronounce as money prompts
them, and they wrap themselves in the robes of the
Lord and say he is with us and no one will dare to
criticize us.

Because of you shall Zion be plowed as an empty field and
Jerusalem shall be a heap of rubble, and the temple
mountain will be a deserted shrine somewhere in the
wilderness.

• • •

6:1–7:7

Listen to what the Lord says. He gets up and he addresses
the jury of the mountains. The hills hear his voice. O
mountains, hear his argument, and you foundations of
the earth, listen to his opening remarks, for the Lord
has a case with his people and he will indict Israel:

O my people, what have I done to you? How have I
wearied you? Say what your complaint may be.

For I brought you out of the land of Egypt and redeemed
you from slavery, and I sent you Moses and Aaron and
Miriam.

Think what Balak, the king of Moab, planned against you,
and remember how Balaam, the son of Beor answered
him and what happened from Shittim to Gilgal. Know
the righteous strength of the Lord.

What is the good of these rituals? You come before the
Lord and bow before the high God with burnt
offerings and yearling calves. Will the Lord be pleased
with thousands of rams or with gallons of oil? Will you
go back to human sacrifice and offer your firstborn
children for your sins?

God has shown you, O man, what is good and what he
wants. What does the Lord require of you? To do
justly, and to love mercy, and to walk humbly with
your God.

The Lord's voice calls out to the city, and men of wisdom
fear his name: Hear, O tribe, and listen, you burghers.
There is the loot of wickedness in the houses of evil
men. There is the skimming of short measure from the
marketplace.

There are rich men who have their wealth from violence
and from falsehood, from the lies of their tongues in
their deceitful mouths.

Therefore, shall I smite you and make you sick, and you
shall be desolate because of your sins. You shall eat but
not be satisfied. You shall be hungry still, and you shall
hoard but have nothing, and what you save will be
taken away by the sword.

You shall sow but never reap. You shall tread olives but
have no oil with which to anoint yourselves. You shall
tread grapes but have no wine to drink.

You are as bad as Omri who kept statues in his house, and
his son Ahab, and you have listened to them and
followed their example. And what I should do is make
you a desolation, your city a wilderness with vipers
hissing from the rocks, and you shall hear them as
scorn and reproaches.

Oh, woe is me, for it is harvest time and there are no grapes
from the vintage; there are no first fruits of summer
that my soul desired, for the good man is perished,
gone from the earth, and there is no upright person
left. They all lie in wait, bloodthirsty, and each man
hunts his brother with a net.

They do evil with both hands. The prince is on the take, the judge has his hand out for a bribe, and the chieftain lets you know his greedy whims. And they are all in cahoots.

The best of them are crooked as a briar bush, the most honest is as sharp as a thorn bush.

The day of your punishment is come, and your watchmen on the walls will announce that the enemy is coming and ruin is at hand.

Do not trust your neighbor, do not rely on your friend. Watch what you say, even to her who lies in your bosom. For the son dishonors the father and the daughter betrays her mother, and the daughter-in-law rebels against her mother-in-law, and your very house is filled with enmity and betrayal.

Look only to the Lord. I will wait for the God of my salvation and pray that God will hear me.

NAHUM

The book of the prophecy of Nahum the Elkoshite, against
Nineveh:

Ardent and vengeful is God, baleful and full of wrath,
raging against his enemies and punishing his
adversaries. He can be long-suffering but is great in
might.

By storms and tempests he makes his way, and a cloud of
dust marks his path.

Chastising the sea, he dries it up and he parches the rivers.

Desiccated are Bashan and Carmel, and the buds of
Lebanon shrivel.

Every mountain quakes in his presence, and the hills all
melt away.

Facing him, the whole earth heaves, the world shudders
and all who dwell in it.

Grievous is his anger. Who can stand before it or endure
the heat of his wrath?

His indignation is fire and its seething shatters the rocks.

In the day of affliction, the Lord is a stronghold and he
knows those who seek in him their place of refuge
from the flood of his retribution.

Justly, he annihilates those who oppose him, pursuing his
enemies into the darkness.

Know then not to scheme against the Lord, for he will
finish you. His enemies do not have a second chance.

Like drunkards they stagger, and there are entangling
thorns everywhere around them, and the thorns are
burning and consumed, like dry stubble.

• • •

The Assyrian will be driven out, he that imagines evil
against the Lord and plots villainy. Thus says the Lord,
for though they be numerous, he will cut them down,
and they will be gone, and report of them will not be
heard again.

I will break this yoke from you and I will shatter your
bonds.

The Lord has given his commandments concerning them,
that their line shall die out and their name shall
disappear. They shall be cut off from their temples
with their carved idols and metal statues. I will prepare
a grave for them, because they are vile.

Look to the mountains: A herald comes to proclaim peace.
You will be able to celebrate the festivals again, O
Judah, and observe the rituals, for the wicked will not
come against you anymore. He is utterly ruined.

2

The disperser is coming up against you. Man the ramparts
and watchtowers. Guard the roads. Gird up your loins
and fortify yourselves,

for the Lord is restoring the magnificence of Jacob that
plunderers have stripped as brigands strip a vineyard.

The shields of his host are red, and his soldiers uniformed in
crimson. Their chariots are drawn up in order,
burnished bright as fire, and their spears shake like the
woods in a wind.

Those chariots shall rattle through the streets jostling one
another in the plazas, and they shall be like torches and
they shall flash by like lightning bolts.

The enemy shall summon his dignitaries who shall stagger
and lean against the walls and try to find places to
hide.

The sluicegates shall open and the palace staff come pouring
out. The princess will be herded along with her
servants and led away, and they shall mourn like doves
and beat their breasts.

Nineveh shall be like a pool of water that drains. "Stop!
Stop!" they shall cry, but none shall stop.

Meanwhile, the invaders will call out "Grab what you can!
Take silver, take gold!" And there shall be no end to
the looting, and plenty of plunder.

And then Nineveh will be empty and desolate and dead,
and their hard hearts will melt, and their knees will
give way, and their loins will be in pain as if they had
been kicked, and their faces will be black with despair.

It was a den of lions, but what is it now? A cave of young
cubs to which the old lion brought his prey. The lion
tore at us for his whelps and strangled us for his
lionesses, and filled his caves with our macerated
flesh.

But behold, I am against you, says the Lord of hosts, and I
will consume your chariots in smoke. My sword shall
destroy your young lions, and there shall be no more
hunting. And the voice of your beaters shall no more
be heard on the earth.

3

Woe to the bloody city, full of lies and endless thieving.
There shall be whips cracking, chariot wheels
rattling, horse hooves pounding and dragging their
battlewagons, and cavalrymen with their swords
glinting and spears shining. There will be piles of
bodies, numberless cadavers in the streets where the
living will stumble over them in their flight.

It is a city of whoring, seductive as any harlot, and ruin
came to all whom she seduced. Nations were ruined
by her wiles and families wrecked by her witchcraft.

Behold, I am therefore against you, says the Lord of hosts.
And I will lift your skirts up over your head and show
all the world your nakedness, and all the kingdoms
will look upon your shame. I will cover you with
stinking ordure and set you up for people to jeer at.

Those who look upon you shall flee and say how utterly
Nineveh is ruined, but no one will be saddened or
surprised. No one will offer comfort to you.

Are you any better than Thebes in Egypt? Protected by the
Nile and fortified, Ethiopia was her ally and Egypt was
her protector, and Libya was her friend. But she is
carried off into captivity, her babies dashed in pieces in
the streets. Her conquerers cast lots for her venerable
men chained on the slave block.

You, too, shall be dazed like a drunkard, and look for a
hole to hide in from your enemy. Your fortresses will
be like fig trees that drop their fruit when anyone
shakes them. You will fall into the mouth of whoever
passes by.

Your soldiers are cowards, are women, and they shall fling
wide the gates and let your enemies in. The timbers
that hold the gates will blaze up and burn away.

Prepare for a siege, store water and fortify your walls. Tread the mortar and bake the bricks in the kiln. It will do no good. The fire will devour you and the sword will cut you down. You will be overrun as by a swarm of locusts.

You are a multitude, but what can you do against the grasshoppers and the locusts? More numerous than the stars, they will swarm over you, and then they will spread their wings and fly away.

Your princes and your scribes, your merchants and your dignitaries, where are they? They, too, are like locusts massed on a wall on a cold morning. When the sun warms them, they will arise as one and fly away, who knows where?

Your shepherds are asleep, O king of Assyria. Your nobles are unconscious. Your people are scattered on the hillsides and there is no one to gather them together.

It is hopeless. There is no healing of this grievous wound. And all who hear of your tribulation shall clap their hands in glee, for whom has your wickedness not afflicted unceasingly?

HABAKKUK

The prophesy of Habakkuk the seer:

How long, O Lord, shall I call out for help and you not
      hear, or cry out against violence, and you not save me?

How can you show me iniquity and make me look upon
      grief?

Destruction and violence are all around me, and strife and
      evil. The law is abandoned and justice, forgotten. The
      wicked overwhelm the good, and the courts are
      corrupt and perverted.

Look among the nations and see, behold in marvel what I
do—a work you would not believe if it were reported
to you. I will raise up the Chaldeans, those barbarians,
and they shall march across the earth and occupy
towns that are not theirs. They are cruel and savage.
They acknowledge no law but their own appetites.

Their horses are faster than leopards, fiercer than ravening
wolves. Their cavalry comes on in pride. Their troops
come from far away, swooping like an eagle that dives
down to its prey.

They come to do violence, and terror precedes them. They
drive their captives as the wind drives the sand,
laughing at kings and scorning all rulers. No
stronghold can resist them, but they come on like the
desert winds, driving the dunes that overwhelm
everything. They sweep by, and their own strength is
their only god.

And where are you, O Lord? Are you not everlasting, my
holy one? We shall not die.

O Lord, you have arraigned them for judgment. O mighty
God, you have indicted them for punishment.

You cannot, with your pure eyes, look upon evil. You
cannot gaze upon wickedness. How can you tolerate
such treachery and keep silent? How can you let these
villains destroy righteous men?

Is mankind no more than the fish of the sea or crawling
   insects, creatures who have no laws and no rulers?
   They fish for them with hooks and drag for them with
   nets, and gather then in their seines, and rejoice and
   exult. They sacrifice to their nets and pray to their
   seines, for they provide them with luxuries and their
   food is sumptuous.

Are they to continue hauling in their nets, merciless as they
   slay the nations of the earth?

2

I will stand watch on the tower and keep alert for what he
   will say to me. I will wait for the answer to my
   complaint and consider how I may then reply.

The Lord answered me with a vision and said write it down
   so that anyone may read it.

The vision bides its time, but in the end it will come. It
   will speak the truth. Wait for its moment, be patient,
   and know that it is on its way inexorably.

For you will behold: He whose soul is corrupted shall
   perish, but the righteous who kept faith shall live.

Wine is a temptation, and pride is treacherous, and appetite
    can be boundless as hell is boundless, unsatisfied as
    Death which can never have enough but gathers to
    itself all nations and all men.

The parables are true and their morals at last hold good, and
    you who expropriate or confiscate and hoard up liens
    and judgments will see your victims suddenly rouse
    themselves and make you their victim, and you will
    tremble in fear.

You have plundered many nations. Will not the remnant of
    their people hate and plunder you?

On your conscience is the blood of men and the violence
    you have done to the earth, and to the cities and those
    who dwell in them.

Woe to him who obtains his house by violence, who sets
    his nest on high where he thinks he is safe from harm.
    You have brought shame to your house and have
    sinned against your souls, cutting off many people.

The stone in the wall will cry out and the beam will answer
    from its place in the woodwork.

Woe to him who builds a town on bloodshed and
    establishes his city on a foundation of iniquity.

Unless it be with the Lord, what the people build will burn
in the fire, and the nations weary themselves in vain,
for the earth will be filled with the knowledge of the
Lord's glory, as the water covers the bed of the sea.

For the violence done to Lebanon, you will be
overwhelmed, and wild beasts will roam the streets
and terrify you.

Woe to him who degrades his neighbor and makes him
drunk and strips him naked. You will be filled with
shame instead of pleasure. If you behave as the
uncircumcised behave, the cup in the Lord's right
hand shall come around to you, and you shall stagger
and vomit in your shame.

What is the good of an idol when its maker has shaped it, a
metal image bitter with lies, for is the workman dumb
who makes the dumb idols? And can he trust in them
himself?

Woe to him who works in wood and stone and says to his
idols, Arise and speak. Teach me.

Even if it be overlaid with gold and silver, there is no
breath in it and no life. But the Lord is in his holy
temple. And before him all the earth is hushed.

3

A prayer of Habakkuk the prophet for the choirmaster:

O Lord, I have heard of what you have done and am in
    awe. Lord, in the worst times, you reveal your true
    self. In your moments of wrath you remember your
    mercy.

In Teman, in Edom, God revealed himself and in the hill
    country between Edom and Sinai, the Holy One
    appeared. His glory covered the skies, and the earth
    was full of his praise. Selah.

His brightness was like light, and martial braids came down
    to his hands. Pestilence went before him, and plague
    followed close behind. He stood and measured the
    earth. He arraigned and tried the nations. The stolid
    mountains fled and the gentle hills bowed low before
    his primitive splendor.

The tents of the tribes of Cushan were shredded and the
    hangings of the Midianites were tattered.

Was the Lord angry with the rivers? Were you displeased
    with the streams and indignant at the ocean? You were
    like a mounted warrior riding his juggernaut car. Your
    bow was strung and your arrows were ready.

You cleaved the earth with rivers. The mountains saw you
and quaked. The waters raged in the riverbeds and
swept on.

The ocean roared and the waves reached up their hands to
you. The sun and moon stopped moving, transfixed
by the arrows of your lightning bolts and your
spearheads of thunder.

You marched through the land in fury and trampled the
heathen in anger. You went forth to save your
people, to save your own anointed. You smote the
heads of the wicked and shattered their skulls with a
rock. Your arrows pierced his chieftains who had
come up like a whirlwind to scatter me and who had
rejoiced in their sneak attacks on our defenseless
people.

You trampled the sea with your steeds churning the mighty
waters.

When I heard what you did, my body trembled and my
lips quivered at the news. My bones turned to jelly
and I quaked in awe: to rest secure in the day of
trouble and know that he will afflict those who
afflict us.

Though the fig tree fail to blossom and the vines neglect to
bear, and though the olive crop fail and the fields yield
no food, and the stalls of the barns be empty, still shall
I rejoice in the Lord and delight in the God of my
salvation.

The Lord God is my strength.

He will make my feet as fleet as the deer's and let me
scamper on the mountain tops.

To the choirmaster, to be sung with stringed instruments.

ZEPHANIAH

The word of the Lord that came to Zephaniah, son of
   Cushi, son of Gedaliah, son of Amariah, son of King
   Hezekiah, in the days of King Josiah, son of Amon,
   King of Judah:

I will sweep the face of the earth clean, says the Lord. I will
   destroy man and beast. I will wipe away the birds of
   the sky and the fish of the sea. I will overthrow the
   wicked. I will obliterate mankind from the face of the
   earth. Thus declares the Lord.

I will point my finger at Judah and against all the
   inhabitants of Jerusalem. And I will expunge from this
   land all those who still worship Báal, and all those who
   burn incense on their rooftops and swear by the Lord
   but pray to the Ammonite's god, Milcom,

and the apostates who have turned away from the Lord, and
those who have not looked to the Lord or prayed to
him.

Hush! before the Lord God, for the day of the Lord is at
hand, and the Lord has prepared a sacrifice and has
sent out invitations, saying that on that chosen day, I
will punish the officials and the princes and all those
who dress themselves in foreign clothing. And I will
punish those who dance in the temple forecourt and in
the Lord's house commit crimes of fraud and even of
violence.

On that day, shall there be a great wailing from the Fish
Gate, a howling from the Mishney quarter, and a loud
crashing sound from The Hills. And those who live
near the quarry shall moan, for the merchants are
finished and the money changers are done for.

When that day comes, I will search Jerusalem with lamps
and punish the men who are settled on their lees and
say in their hearts, "The Lord does me no good but
neither does he do me any harm."

Their goods shall be plundered and their houses emptied
and ruined. They shall build homes but not live in
them, and they shall plant vineyards but not drink any
wine they produce.

The great day of the Lord is approaching, and it comes on
faster than a runner. The voice of the Lord shall be
heard, and the voice of mighty men crying bitterly, for
that day will be a day of wrath and anguish and
trouble and ruin and devastation, a day of darkness and
of gloom, a day thick with black clouds and trumpet
blasts and battle cries against the fortified cities with
their lofty towers.

I will bring suffering to men so that they shall walk about as
if blind because they have sinned against the Lord.
Their blood shall spill out into the dust and their flesh
will be like shit.

Their silver and gold will not save them on that day of the
Lord's wrath. In the fire of his anger all the earth shall
be consumed, for he will make a quick end to all the
inhabitants of the earth and good riddance to them.

2

Gather yourselves together, O brazen nation, and call a
conclave before you are scattered away like chaff,
before the fierce anger of the Lord comes down
upon you, before the day of God's wrath descends
upon you.

And you, the meek of the earth who obey his commandments, seek the Lord and rely on justice and humility. You may be hidden in safety on that day of the wrath of the Lord, for Gaza will be emptied and Ashkelon shall be a desolate place, and in Ashdod at high noon there shall not be a living soul, and Ekron shall be deserted.

Woe to those who live along the seacoast, you nation of Philistines. The word of the Lord has been spoken against you. O Canaan, land of the Philistines, I will destroy you and there shall not be an inhabitant left.

The seacoast will be empty pasture land for shepherds and their grazing flocks. And the coast shall be the possession of the remnant of the house of Judah, and they shall pasture there and lie down in the evening in the abandoned houses of Ashkelon, for the Lord their god shall save them and restore them to prosperity.

I have heard the propaganda of Moab and the insults of the children of Ammon. They have reviled my people and looked to expand their lands and encroach on my people's borders. Therefore, as I live, says the Lord of hosts, the God of Israel, surely Moab shall be like Sodom and the children of Ammon shall be like Gomorrah. Their territory will be a field of nettles, barren, a perpetual desert, and my people shall despoil them of whatever they have, and the remnant of my people shall possess what they once had.

This is the punishment for their pride, because they boasted
and jeered at the people of the Lord of hosts. The
Lord will be terrible to them. He will impoverish all
the earth's godlings so that all men of all nations shall
worship only him and each man in his home shall bow
down to him alone.

And you, the people of Cush, shall be slain by the sword.
And the Lord will point to the north and destroy
Assyria and he will make Nineveh a desert wasteland.

In what is now the city square, flocks shall lie down to
chew the cud and all manner of wild beasts shall roam.
The owl shall hoot in the empty windows and the
bittern shall nest on the lintels. The raven shall croak
on the threshold and its cawing shall resound on the
wooden floors.

This is what will happen to the braggart city that said in her
heart, "Who is like me?" She will be nothing but a
desolation, a barn in which beasts take shelter, and
passers-by shall look and shake their heads and hiss in
their derision.

3

Shame on this foul city, polluted and tyrannical.

She listens to no one and accepts no correction. She does
not trust in the Lord or approach her God. Her
potentates are roaring lions and her judges are wolves
that come prowling in the evening and leave nothing
alive at dawn. Her prophets are frivolous, faithless
men, and her priests profane what should be sacred
and do violence to the law.

But the Lord does no iniquity. Each morning he shows
forth the light of his judgment which is sure as the
dawn. Still, the unjust know no shame.

I have cut down nations. Their fortifications are in ruins.
Their streets grow wild and no one walks there. Their
cities are destroyed and abandoned and no one lives
there.

I said, Surely Judah will fear me, taking instruction and
receiving correction, so that they may not be likewise
cut down. But they rose early and hustled to their
corruption.

But wait and see, says the Lord, for the day when I rise up
to strike, for I am resolved to gather the nations and
assemble the kingdoms and pour out on them my
wrath and the heat of my anger. All the earth shall be
consumed by the fire of my rage.

I will purify the speech of the people so that all of them call
upon the name of the Lord and serve him with one
breath.

From beyond the rivers of Africa, my suppliants shall bring
me offerings, and the daughters of my scattered people
will come to pray.

In that day, you shall not be humiliated because of your
evil deeds by which you transgressed against me. I
shall remove from your midst those wicked men who
were proud and overbearing, and they shall no longer
strut on Zion. But the humble and the poor shall be
left alone and shall trust in the name of the Lord.
Those who are left in Israel shall have the Lord as
their refuge, and they shall do no wrong and speak
no lies. There will not be a deceitful tongue in any of
their mouths, for they shall be my flock and shall
graze and lie down in safety and none shall threaten
them.

Sing, then, O daughter of Zion, and shout O Israel.

    Rejoice and be glad with all your heart, O daughter of Jerusalem.

The Lord has canceled his judgments against you and has cast out your enemies. The King of Israel reigns over you and you shall not fear evil anymore.

On that day, it shall be said to Jerusalem, Do not fear. And to Zion, Do not give up hope. The Lord will rejoice in your gladness and refresh you with his love. He will exult over you with loud song.

I will gather your hurt and wounded and take away the burden of their reproach.

I will remedy your affliction and punish your oppressors, and I will save the lame and welcome the outcast, and I will change their shame into fame and praise in every land on earth. I will bring you home again and make a name for you, and when I gather you together you will be renowned among the peoples of the earth. I will undo your captivity, says the Lord, and restore your good fortune.

HAGGAI

In the second year of the reign of King Darius, on the first
day of the month of Elul, the word of the Lord came
through Haggai the prophet to Zerubbabel, the son of
Shealtiel, the governor of Judah, and to Joshua, the
son of Josedech, the high priest, and he said, Thus says
the Lord of Hosts:

The people say that the time has not come to rebuild the
Lord's house. But the word of the Lord came to
Haggai the prophet, asking how you have had time to
build your wainscoted houses while this house lies in
ruins.

The Lord of hosts bids you consider your condition. You
have sown much but harvested little. You eat but
never have your fill. You drink but your thirst is not
slaked. You clothe yourselves but shiver in the cold.
You earn your wages only to put them in a pocket
with holes.

Consider your condition, says the Lord of hosts. Go up to
the hill country and fetch lumber to build the temple,
that I may take pleasure in it and bask in my glory,
says the Lord.

You have expected much but realized little, for whatever
you brought home blew away. Why, the Lord asks?
Because my house lies in ruins while each of you
labors on his own house. Therefore, the heavens above
you have withheld the dew and the earth has withheld
its yield. I have ordered a drought on the fields and
the hillsides, and there is no grain or new wine or oil.
There is a dearth of what the earth brings forth with
the labor of men and beasts.

Then Zerubbabel, the son of Shealtiel, and Joshua the son
of Josedech the high priest, with all the remnant of the
people obeyed the voice of the Lord their God and the
words of Haggai the prophet whom the Lord had sent,
and the people were in awe before the Lord.

Then Haggai, the Lord's messenger, spoke to the people,
telling them the Lord says, I am with you.

And the Lord roused the spirit of Zerubbabel, the son of
Shealtiel, governor of Judah, and the spirit of Joshua
the son of Josedech, the high priest, and the spirits of
all the remnant of the people, and they came and did
the work in the house of the Lord of hosts, their God
on the twenty-fourth day of the sixth month in the
second year of the reign of King Darius.

2

In the second year of the reign of King Darius on the
twenty-first day of the month of Tishri, the word of
the Lord came through Haggai the prophet: Speak
now to Zerubbabel, the son of Shealtiel, governor of
Judah, and the spirit of Joshua the son of Josedech, the
high priest, and to all the remnant of the people and
say, Who is left among you that saw this house in its
former glory? And how do you see it now? Does it not
look insignificant?

The Lord says, Be strong O Zerubbabel, and persevere, O
Joshua son of Josedech, the high priest. Apply
yourselves, all you people of the land, the Lord says.
Work, says the Lord of hosts, for I am with you.

Once again will I shake the heavens and the earth and the
    sea and the dry land, and I will make all the nations
    quake so that the treasures of all the world will come
    to fill this house with splendor, says the Lord of hosts.
    The silver is mine and the gold is mine, the Lord says.
    The splendor of this house that will be must be greater
    than the splendor that was, the Lord says, and in this
    place I will bestow prosperity.

In the twenty-fourth day of the month of Kislev in the
    second year of the reign of King Darius, the word of
    the Lord came through Haggai, the prophet,
    announcing, Thus says the Lord of Hosts:

If a man carries a consecrated victim to the altar in the skirt
    of his garment, and the garment then touches bread or
    soup or wine or oil or any other kind of food, does
    that then become holy? And the priests answered, No.

Then Haggai said, If one who is unclean having touched a
    corpse touch any of these things, do they become
    unclean? And the priests answered, Yes, they become
    unclean.

And Haggai then said, So it is with the people and with this
    nation before me, the Lord says, with the work of
    their hands. What they offer is unclean.

I charge you, think about what your condition will be from
this day forward. Before a stone was placed upon a
stone, how were you doing?

You went to the storehouse where you had put by twenty
measures, but you found only ten. You went to your
wine vat where you had put by fifty measures but you
found only twenty. I afflicted you and all the fruit of
your labors with blight and mildew and hail. But you
did not return to me, says the Lord.

Think about this day onward, from the twenty-fourth day
of Kislev. Since the day that the foundation of the
Lord's temple was laid, think. Is there any seed left in
the barn? Does the vine yield anything? Or the fig
tree? Or the pomegranate, or the olive? But from this
day on, I will bless you.

And again on the twenty-fourth day of the month, the
word of the Lord came to Haggai, saying, Speak to
Zerubbabel, governor of Judah, saying I will shake the
heavens and the earth, the sea and the dry land. I will
overthrow the thrones of kingdoms and destroy the
strength of the nations of the heathen. I will overturn
their chariots and those who ride in them, and their
horses and riders shall fall, each one of them, by the
sword of his brother.

In that day, says the Lord of hosts, I will take you,
    Zerubbabel, my servant, the son of Shealtiel, and make
    you like a signet ring, for I have elected you, says the
    Lord of hosts.

ZECHARIAH

In the eighth month in the second year of the reign of
Darius the word of the Lord came to the prophet
Zechariah, son of Berechiah, the son of Iddo, saying,
The Lord has been angry with your fathers. Therefore
tell them that the Lord says if they will return to me, I
will return to them.

Do not do as your fathers did. The old prophets cried to
them saying that the Lord of hosts orders them to end
their evil ways and stop their wrongdoing. But they
would not hear and they did not pay attention.

Your fathers are dead and those prophets are dead. They do not live forever, but my words and the laws I commanded my priests and prophets to convey are still good. Did they not catch up with your fathers? And they repented and acknowledged that the Lord of hosts did to them according to what they deserved and dealt fairly with them.

On the twenty-fourth day of the month of Shebat, in the second year of the reign of Darius, the word of the Lord came to the prophet Zechariah, son of Berechiah, the son of Iddo, saying, I looked out into the night and saw an angel riding a red horse. He was standing among the myrtle trees in the valley and behind them were other riders on red and white and dappled horses.

And I said, What, sir, are these? And the angel spoke to me and said he would explain them. These are the ones the Lord has sent to patrol the earth. And they answered the angel of the Lord standing among the myrtle trees and said, We have roamed through the earth and behold the whole earth sits still and is at rest.

Then the angel of the Lord said, O Lord of hosts, how long
will you be harsh to Jerusalem and the cities of Judah
at which you have been angry for seventy years now?
The Lord answered the angel with gracious and
comforting words who then spoke to me saying, Pray.
The Lord says, I am jealous for Jerusalem and for Zion
and I am greatly angered with the heathen that are so
comfortable.

I had been annoyed with Judah but their punishment was
greater than what was required. And therefore, the
Lord says, I feel compassion again for Jerusalem. My
house shall be built in it and surveyors' lines shall be
drawn for the rebuilding of its ruins.

Proclaim it again, the Lord of hosts says, for the cities of
Judah shall once more enjoy prosperity and the Lord
will comfort Zion and choose Jerusalem again.

Then I raised my eyes and what I saw was four horns. And
I said to the angel who was explaining things to me,
What are these? And he said, These are the four
directions from which the nations have come to scatter
Judah, Israel, and Jerusalem.

And the Lord showed me four smiths, and I asked, What
are they coming to do? And the angel answered, these
are the horns that scattered Judah, so that no man
could hold his head up, but these men are come to
cast down the horns of the nations who lifted up their
horns against the land of Judah to disperse it.

2

I looked up again and I saw a man with a measuring line in
his hand, and I asked, Where are you going? And he
said, To measure Jerusalem to see how broad it is and
how long.

And see, the angel that had talked with me went forward
and another angel joined him and said to him, Run
and tell this young man that Jerusalem shall be like a
town without walls for all the men and women and
cattle who live there. For the Lord says, I will be like a
wall of fire protecting her and I will be the glory that
shines from within her.

Ho, there, come back from the lands of the north, the Lord
says, for I have scattered you abroad with the four
winds of heaven. But escape now to Zion, you who
live with the daughter of Babylon.

Thus says the Lord of hosts whose glory has sent me to the
nations who despoiled you. For whoever touches you
touches the apple of his eye.

Watch, I will shake my hand over them and they shall be
the victims of those they victimized, and then you
shall know for certain that the Lord of hosts has sent
me.

Sing and rejoice, daughter of Zion, for I have come to you,
the Lord says, and I will dwell among you. And from
many nations you shall join yourselves to the Lord on
that day, and the Lord will inherit Judah as his legacy
in the holy land and he shall choose Jerusalem again.

Be silent, all mortal flesh, before the Lord, for he has roused
himself from his heavenly dwelling.

3

And he showed me Joshua the high priest standing before
the angel of the Lord, and Satan was standing at his
right hand to oppose him. And the Lord said to Satan,
The Lord rebukes you, O Satan. The Lord who has
chosen Jerusalem rebukes you. Is this man not a brand
plucked from the fire?

Now Joshua was wearing filthy clothing as he stood before
the angel. And the angel spoke to all those present
saying, Take away his filthy clothes. And to Joshua he
said, See, I have removed your iniquity from you, and
I will clothe you with rich new apparel. Put a clean
turban on his head. And they did so, and the angel of
the Lord stood by. And the angel said to Joshua, Thus
says the Lord of hosts. If you walk in my ways and
keep my commandments, then you shall rule my
house and be in charge of my courts, and I will give
you authority over those who are standing here.

Hear now, Joshua, the high priest, you and your friends are
men of good omen. See how I will bring forth my
servant, the scion of David.

And see the stone I have set before Joshua. On one stone
shall be seven characters, and I will engrave the stone
with an inscription, says the Lord of hosts, and I will
remove the guilt of the land in one day, and you shall
call every man your neighbor, and each man shall sit
in peace under his vine and beneath his fig tree.

4

And the angel who talked with me came again and woke
   me up, as a man is awakened from a deep sleep, and
   he said to me, What do you see? I said, I see a
   candelabrum of gold with a bowl on its top and seven
   lamps, and on each of them seven lips for the wicks.
   And there are two olive trees, one on the right side of
   the candelabrum and one on the left.

And I asked the angel, What are these, sir? The angel
   replied, Do you not know what they are? I said, No,
   sir, and he said to me, This is the word of the Lord to
   Zerubbabel: Not by might or by force shall you rule,
   but by my spirit, says the Lord of hosts.

What are you, O steep mountainside? Zerubbabel shall
   climb you and walk as easily as upon a plain. And he
   shall set the temple cornerstone in place among shouts
   of Splendid! How splendid it is!

The word of the Lord came to me, saying, The hands of
   Zerubbabel have laid the foundation of my house. His
   hands shall finish it too, and then you shall know that
   the Lord of hosts has sent me to you. For he who has
   despised this day of small things shall rejoice and shall
   see the plumb line in the hand of Zerubbabel.

These seven lamps are the eyes of the Lord that range over the whole earth. And I asked him what are the two olive trees to the right and left of the candelabrum? And I asked again, What do the trees mean that are beside the golden spouts from which the oil pours out? And he said, Do you now know what they are? I said, No, sir. And he said, These are the two anointed who stand by the Lord of the whole earth.

5

Then I looked up and saw overhead a flying scroll, and he asked me, What do you see? And I said, I see a flying scroll, thirty feet long and fifteen feet wide. And he said, This is the curse that goes out over the face of the earth, and everyone who steals shall be ostracized and everyone who swears falsely shall be cut off, as it is inscribed on that scroll. I will send it forth and it shall enter the house of the thief and the man who swears falsely by my name, and it shall stay there in the midst of his house and consume his house, timber and stone.

Then the angel who talked to me said, Now look up and see what obtains. And I asked, What is it? And he said, It is a bushel basket. This is their iniquity throughout the earth. And they removed the leaden cover of the basket and there was a woman sitting in it. And the angel said, This is wickedness, and he thrust her back into the basket and put the leaden cover back on it.

Then I raised my eyes and looked, and I saw two women
who had wings like storks', and the wind was in their
wings and they lifted up the basket and flew with it
between the earth and the heavens. And I asked the
angel, Where are they taking the bushel basket? And
he said, To the land of Shinar, to build a temple for it,
and when this is ready, they will set the basket there
upon its altar.

6

I turned and raised my eyes and looked, and I saw four
chariots that came down from between two
mountains, and the mountains were of bronze. The
first chariot had red horses, and the second had black
horses, and the third had white horses, and the fourth
had dappled gray horses. And I asked the angel who
talked with me, What, sir, are these?

The angel answered and told me, These are the spirits of
the four winds of heaven which come from the Lord
and go forth to all the earth. The red horses go to the
east country, and black horses go to the north country,
and the white go west, and the dappled ones go south.

When these steeds came forth, they were impatient to range
over the earth, and he said, Go patrol the earth, and so
they did, running over the earth. Then he cried out to
me, Those who go to the north country, to Babylon,
have set my spirit at rest there.

And the word of the Lord came to me, saying, Take silver
and gold from the exiles Heldai, and Tobijah, and
Jedaiah, who have arrived from Babylon, and go
immediately to the house of Josiah, the son of
Zephaniah. And with the silver and gold they have
brought make a crown of it, and set it on the head of
Joshua, son of Jehosedech, the high priest, and
announce to him, Thus says the Lord of hosts. Behold
the man whose name is the scion of David, for he shall
grow up in his place and shall build the temple of the
Lord.

It is he who shall build the temple of the Lord and rule on
his throne. And there shall be a priest by the throne
and there shall be peace between them both.

And the crown shall be in the temple of the Lord as a
reminder of Heldai, and Tobijah, and Jedaiah, and
Josiah, the son of Zephaniah. And those who are far
away shall come to help build the temple of the Lord.
And you shall know that the Lord of hosts has sent me
to you. And all this shall come to pass if you obey
diligently the words of the Lord your God.

7

And it came to pass in the fourth year of the reign of King
Darius that the word of the Lord came to Zechariah in
the fourth day of Kislev. Now Bethel sent El-sharezer,
the chief officer of the king, and his men, to beg the
favor of the Lord and to ask the priests of the Temple
of the Lord of hosts and the prophets, Should I mourn
and fast in the fifth month, as I have done for so many
years to commemorate the destruction of the temple?

Then the word of the Lord came to me and told me, Ask
the people of the land and ask the priests whether it
was for me that they fasted and mourned in the fifth
month and in the seventh, for these past seventy years.

When you eat, do you not eat for yourselves? And when
you drink, do you not drink for yourselves?

When Jerusalem was populous and prosperous and the cities
around her thrived, and the lowlands in the Negev
were inhabited, were not these the words the Lord
proclaimed through the prophets of that time? Did the
Lord not say, Render true judgments, show kindness
and be merciful each man to his brother? Do not
oppress the widow or the orphan or the traveler or the
pauper, and let none of you devise evil in your heart
against your fellow man.

But they did not listen and they turned a cold shoulder and
stopped their ears that they might not hear. They
made their hearts as hard as stones lest they should hear
the law and the words that the Lord of hosts had sent
by his Spirit through the prophets of those times.

Therefore, a great anger arose in the Lord of hosts. As I
called, they would not hear, so they may call now and
I will not hear, said the Lord of hosts. And I scattered
them with a whirlwind among the nations they had
not known and left their land desolate so that no one
moved and their rich countryside was a desert.

8

And the word of the Lord came again to me, saying, I am
jealous for Zion with a great jealousy and jealous for
her with a great anger. I will return to Zion and will
dwell in Jerusalem, and Jerusalem shall be called the
faithful city and Zion shall be called the holy
mountain.

Thus says the Lord of hosts, Old men and old women shall sit again in the streets of Jerusalem with their walking sticks in their hands. And the streets of the city shall be full of boys and girls playing. Even though it seems impossible to the remnant of the people in these days, and even if it should seem impossible even to me, says the Lord of hosts, yet will I save my people from Babylon and from Egypt, and I will bring them to dwell in Jerusalem where they shall be my people and I will be their God, in faithfulness and righteousness.

Thus says the Lord of Hosts, Let your hands be strong, you who have heard these words from the mouth of the prophets since the day that the foundation of the temple of the Lord of hosts was laid so that the house of the Lord might be built. In days gone by, there was no wage for the laborer and his beast, nor safety from the foe for any man who went out of his house or came home to it, for I set every man against his fellow. But now I will relent and I will not be to the survivors of this people as I was in former days. For there shall be a sowing of peace and prosperity. The vine shall produce its grapes and the ground shall give its yield, and the heavens shall send down their dew, and I will cause the survivors of this people to possess all these things.

As you have been a byword of contempt among the
nations, O Judah and Israel, so shall your name now be
a blessing. Do not be afraid, but let your hands be
strong.

For the Lord of hosts says, I thought to punish you when
your forebears provoked me to anger, and I did not
repent. So have I thought again in these days to do
well by Jerusalem and to the house of Judah. Do not
doubt it.

These are the things you must do: Let every man speak the
truth to his neighbor. Execute judgments of truth and
peace in your dwellings. Do not devise evil against
your neighbors. And hate false swearing. For these are
the things that I hate, says the Lord.

And the word of the Lord of hosts came to me saying, The
fast of the fourth month and the fast of the fifth, and of
the seventh, and of the tenth month shall be seasons of
joy and gladness to the house of Judah, times of
feasting. Therefore love truth and peace.

This is what the Lord of hosts says: Peoples shall come from
many cities, and the inhabitants of one city shall travel
to another, saying, Let us go to beg the favor of the
Lord and seek the Lord of hosts. I am going, myself.
Many people and nations shall come to seek the Lord
of hosts in Jerusalem and to beg the Lord's favor. Thus
says the Lord of hosts: In those days, ten men from the
nations of every language shall take hold of the robe of
each Jew and ask, Let us accompany you for we have
heard that God is with you.

MALACHI

The message of the Lord to Israel through Malachi:

The Lord says, I have loved you, and you say, How? And
    the Lord asks, Wasn't Esau Jacob's brother? And I
    loved Jacob and hated Esau. I have turned his hill
    country into a wilderness and given his heritage to the
    jackals.

And if the Edomites say they will come back and rebuild
    their desolate places, the Lord answers that he will
    destroy them again and people will call that region the
    badlands. And men shall know that the Edomites are
    the people the Lord hates forever. You shall see this
    with your own eyes, and you shall say the Lord is great
    not only in Israel but beyond.

A son honors his father and a servant respects his master. If I am a father, where is my honor? And if I am a master, where is my respect? That is what the Lord of hosts asks of you, O priests who dishonor his name. And the priests ask, How have we dishonored his name? By offering polluted food on the Lord's altar. And you ask, How is it polluted? The Lord knows what you think—that it makes no difference what you offer him.

You offer blind animals for sacrifice. Is this not contemptuous? You offer lame and sick animals. Is this not wicked? Try such a thing with your governors and see if they be pleased with you or accept your gifts, says the Lord of hosts.

But this is how you approach the Lord to ask for his favor and pray that he be gracious to us. How do you suppose he will respond?

There should be one of you who could understand that it is better to shut the doors of the temple than to kindle fires on my altars for such vain sacrifices. I have no pleasure in them and I will not accept such offerings from your hands.

From the east where the sun rises to the west where it sets, my name shall be great among the gentiles and in every place incense shall be offered to my name and kosher offerings, for my name shall be great among the heathen, says the Lord of hosts.

But you profane my name when you pollute the table of
the Lord here in Jerusalem, and when the offerings to
the Lord are contemptible.

You say it is tiresome, and you sniff at me, says the Lord,
and you bring wounded animals and lame and sick as
your offerings. Shall I accept such gifts from your
hand?

The deceiver shall be cursed who promises to sacrifice a
male animal to the Lord and then, when the time
comes to fulfill his promise, brings a blemished beast, a
corrupt thing. For I am a great king, says the Lord of
hosts, and my name is feared among the nations.

2

And now, priests, this message is for you. If you will not
listen and do not take it to heart to give glory to my
name, says the Lord of hosts, then I will send my curse
upon you and I will turn your blessings to curses.
Indeed, I have already done so, because you do not
mean in your hearts what you say with your mouths.

I will make the land barren and I will cover your faces with
dung, the ordure of your offerings, and banish you
from my presence as unclean.

Know that I have sent this commandment to you. It does
not violate my covenant with Levi, for that was a
covenant of life and peace that I gave him that he
might hold me in awe, and he did stand in awe of my
name, and falsehood was not found on his lips. He
walked with me in peace and honor and turned away
from sin.

For the lips of a priest should keep secrets, and men should
seek instruction from his mouth, for he is the
messenger of the Lord of hosts. But you have turned
away from me and your instruction has caused many
to stumble. You have broken the covenent of Levi,
says the Lord of hosts, and I shall show you up as
contemptible and despicable before all my people
because you have not been faithful and observant and
have been corrupt in your administration of the law.

Are we not all the children of one father? Did not the one
God create us all? Then why are we faithless to one
another, and why do we profane the covenant of our
fathers?

Judah has been treacherous and Israel has committed
abominations in Jerusalem. Judah has profaned the
sanctuary of the Lord which he loves and has
worshipped strange gods the way some men fall in
love with foreign women.

But the Lord will cut off the man who does this, rabbi or
  scholar, banishing him from the tabernacles of Jacob,
  and he shall have no standing in our courts and shall
  not be allowed to bring offerings to the Lord of hosts.

You keep on doing this, covering the Lord's altar with
  tears, weeping and moaning because he no longer
  finds your offerings acceptable and is unwilling to
  receive them from your hand. And you ask, Why not?

Because you have been faithless to the wife of your youth
  with whom you made a covenant, although she still
  loves you and your covenant still holds.

Why then should the Lord keep the covenant he made
  with us to sustain us and keep us in the spirit of life?

What does he desire of us? Godly children. So wake up,
  pay attention, and let none be faithless to the wife of
  his youth. For the Lord, God of Israel, says, I hate
  divorce. You cannot abandon your wife like an old
  garment you put aside. So take care of your soul's
  health and do not be faithless.

You have exhausted the patience of the Lord with your talk
  and you wonder, How have we wearied him? By
  proclaiming that those who do evil are good in the
  sight of the Lord and that he delights in them. You
  have lost your faith in the God of justice.

3

Behold, I will send my messenger and he shall prepare the
path before me, and the Lord you seek shall appear in
his temple, the messenger of the covenant of which
you are proud. Behold, says the Lord of hosts, he is
coming.

But who shall be able to stand it when he comes and who
shall endure it when he appears and judges. For he is
like a refiner's fire or like a fuller's bleach. He shall sit
as a smelter of silver and purify the sons of Levi,
purging them as goldsmiths do to silver and gold, so
that they may make offerings to the Lord in
righteousness.

Then shall the offerings of Judah in Jerusalem be pleasing to
the Lord as in days of old and years gone by.

The Lord of hosts says, Then I will come near to you to
judge. I will be a forthcoming witness against sorcerers
and adulterers and false swearers, and those who cheat
hired workers of their wages, or defraud widows and
orphans, or are unwelcoming to strangers, and who do
not fear me.

For I am the Lord and I do not change. Because of my
patience, you sons of Jacob have not been destroyed.
From the days of your forebears, you have broken my
laws and ignored them. The Lord of hosts says, Return
to me, and I will return to you.

And you ask, How shall we return?

Will a man swindle God? You have swindled me. You ask,
How? In tithes and offerings.

You are cursed with a terrible curse, because you have
swindled me and the entire nation.

Bring all those tithes into the storehouse that there may be
food in my house. Try me, says the Lord of hosts, and
see if I do not open the windows of heaven to you and
pour out my overflowing blessings upon you. I will
punish the locust so it shall not destroy your crops in
the field, and your vines will not lose their fruit before
it ripens. And the nations shall call you blessed, for
yours will be a delightful land.

You have spoken harshly against me, says the Lord. And
you ask, How have we done that?

You have said it is pointless to serve God. What is the good
in observing his commandments or walking in
mourning before the Lord of hosts?

We look at arrogant men and call them happy. Those who
do wickedness prosper. They tempt God and get away
with it.

Those who believed in the Lord and held him in awe spoke
to one another, and the Lord heard and a book of
remembrance was written down in which those who
feared the Lord and thought of his name were
inscribed.

They shall be mine, says the Lord of hosts, my prized
possessions on that day when I strike, but I will spare
them as a man spares his own son who serves him.
Then once again you shall be able to distinguish
between the righteous and the wicked, between one
who serves God and one who does not.

4

For, see, the day comes, hot as an oven, and all the proud
and all the wicked shall be stubble and that day that
comes shall burn them, says the Lord of hosts, and it
shall leave them neither root nor branch. But for you
who fear my name, the sun of righteousness shall rise
with healing in its rays, and you shall go forth and
grow like calves leaping from their stalls.

You shall tread down the wicked. On the day when I act, they shall be ashes under the soles of your shoes.

Remember the laws of my servant, Moses, the statutes and the edicts that I commanded him at Horeb for all Israel.

Watch! I will send you Elijah the prophet before that great and terrible day arrives. He shall turn the hearts of fathers to their children and the hearts of children to their fathers, lest I come and strike the earth with a curse.